The Wh...
Cookbook

Caroline Liddell

Illustrated by Sharon Finmark

CORONET BOOKS
Hodder and Stoughton.

Copyright © 1980 by Caroline Liddell

First published in Great Britain 1980
by Coronet Books
Second impression 1981

British Library C.I.P.

The wholefoods cookbook.
   1. Cookery (Natural foods)
   641.5'63   TX741

   ISBN 0–340–25454–8

Printed and bound in Great Britain for
Hodder and Stoughton Paperbacks, a
division of Hodder and Stoughton Ltd.,
Mill Road, Dunton Green, Sevenoaks,
Kent (Editorial Office: 47 Bedford
Square, London, WC1 3DP) by
Richard Clay (The Chaucer Press) Ltd,
Bungay, Suffolk

THE WHOLEFOODS COOKBOOK

Caroline Liddell has wide experience
of professional cookery and has worked
closely with both Delia Smith and Robert
Carrier.

She has long been interested in wholefoods
and wanted particularly to compile a collection
of recipes which would fill the gap on everyone's
shelves: a wholefood cookbook that
combines both healthy eating *and* an expert,
imaginative knowledge of the art.

There is a wide variety of recipes ranging
from soups to baking and tasty ideas for both
the meat-eater and the vegetarian, the
poverty-stricken and the rich, the dilettante
and the committed enthusiast: all, in fact, who
enjoy nourishing, delicious meals.

To D and M without whom . . .

CONTENTS

FOREWORD

I cheerfully own up to the fact that there is no philosophy or crusade behind the writing of this book other than the sheer pleasure I get from eating wholefoods and the wish to communicate this pleasure to others.

The weight of medical findings would indicate that there are strong reasons for eating wholefoods. We are told that roughage in the Western diet is at an all time low, to the ruination of our intestinal tracts. And when roughage is mentioned you can be sure that cholesterol and sugar will not be far behind.

Quite frankly, I simply cannot work up a sweat about all this. The plain truth is that we all eat too much. Then what on earth are you doing writing a cookery book, I hear you cry? Simply, I believe in *quality*. Since most of us should be eating only about half our present consumption, I suggest that we exercise our culinary skills and ingenuity to the utmost to make the most of what is left, and produce really delicious meals from what is good for us.

INTRODUCTION

by Delia Smith

There are two reasons why I am enthusiastic about this book. One is that I'm more and more convinced about the value of wholefoods in our everyday diet. Nutritionally the evidence is very sound and, increasingly, I am finding both the flavour and texture of 'whole' foods to be so much better than the refined and processed equivalents we've got into the habit of eating.

Commercialism has a great deal to answer for: a large part of our modern diet has become so bland and boring. But at least—thanks to the pioneers of the wholefoods movement—we do now have some sort of choice, at any rate so far as home cooking is concerned. Hopefully, in the future, perhaps even restaurants and mass catering establishments will offer the same sort of choice.

The second reason for my enthusiasm is the book's author, Caroline Liddell, whose cooking mind and instincts are so very similar to my own. Indeed, we worked together for several years and her ideas and inspiration have provided a great deal of backbone to my own collection of recipes.

This, her first solo, is precisely what I'd expected and what has been much needed: a collection of recipes which puts the everyday use of wholefoods into that 'something special' bracket. Hitherto this back-to-the-earth subject has often been treated simply as *down*-to-earth, and its proponents have tackled it from the health point of view without a great deal of cooking knowledge.

Now, at last, we have a wholefoods cookery book with plenty of culinary flair. I hope you all enjoy the recipes as much as I have.

CONVERSION TABLES

WEIGHTS

½ oz	10 g (grams)
1	25
1½	40
2	50
2½	60
3	75
4	110
4½	125
5	150
6	175
7	200
8	225
9	250
10	275
12	350
1 lb	450
1½	700
2	900
3	1 kg 350 g

VOLUME

2 fl oz	55 ml
3 fl oz	75
5 fl oz (¼ pint)	150
½ pint	275
¾ pint	425
1 pint	570
1¾ pints	1 litre
(2-pint basin = 1 litre)	

TEMPERATURES

Mark 1	275 °F	140 °C
2	300	150
3	325	170
4	350	180
5	375	190
6	400	200
7	425	220
8	450	230

MEASUREMENTS

⅛ in	3 mm (millimetre)
¼ in	½ cm (centimetre)
½	1
¾	2
1	2·5
1¼	3
1½	4
1¾	4·5
2	5
3	7·5
4	10
5	13
6	15
7	18
8	20
9	23
10	25·5
11	28
12	30

All these are *approximate* conversions, which have been either rounded up or down. In a few recipes it has been necessary to modify them very slightly.

SOME NOTES
FOR THE COOK

KITCHEN EQUIPMENT

Since this is a cookery book written for reasonably keen, proficient cooks, the following list consists only of a few items which are of particular help in tackling the recipes.

Measuring Spoons

I have given up the unequal struggle of getting people to use a standard set of measuring spoons, so use a plain, ordinary, orthodox size of teaspoon, dessertspoon and tablespoon, and make the measurements in these level, unless otherwise indicated by the recipe.

Liquidiser

This is a marvellous invention for the cook, although I must admit that nowadays I tend to get a little tired of the uniform pap that these machines inevitably produce and am now coming down more in favour of good, old-fashioned moulis.

Moulis

There is the large model with three grinding plates ranging from coarse to fine, and a small drum model which is excellent for grinding cheese and nuts.

Sieves

It is worth investing in the sturdiest ones available, in a range of sizes, both metal and nylon. Put all fruits, or anything that tends to be acidic, through the nylon sieves; the metal ones can take care of the rest.

Pressure Cooker

Mine certainly earns its keep, but they do seem to terrify a lot of people. Worth it, I think, even if only used to cut down the time it takes to cook dried pulses; but it is also excellent for home-made stocks.

Lemon Zester

This is something I find I am using more and more in the kitchen, purely because it is far easier to wash up a zester than an enormous grater. And I prefer the slightly chunkier strips of citrus-fruit zest, which can be used in cakes and puddings, etc., or as decorations.

Pestle and Mortar

The ceramic ones are the best. No matter how pretty the glass or wooden ones may be, they will not prove as satisfactory as the ceramic in the long run. Also, buy one of a reasonable size, about 570 ml (1 pint) capacity. They are very useful for crushing all kinds of herbs, spices, salt and garlic in a way a liquidiser never can. Spoons and rolling pins are poor substitutes.

INGREDIENTS

Salt

There are three choices open to you: (**a**) table salt (**b**) rock salt (**c**) sea salt.

Table salt is refined and made free-running by the addition of magnesium carbonate, which upsets a lot of people who prefer their food unadulterated. It cannot be used for curing because of the presence of this and other chemicals.

Rock salt comes mainly from the Cheshire mines. It is slightly coarser than kitchen or table salt.

Sea salt is evaporated either by artificial heat or by the sun.

For me, salt is salt. The only occasion when any subtle difference is apparent is when salt comes to the palate at its most unsullied—that is, when you add it to the food at the table. For this purpose I recommend a sun-dried sea salt sprinkled over the food with the fingers.

Pepper

A peppermill is a must in every kitchen. Pepper bought ready ground has already lost some of its fragrance and strength. The dried black berries (peppercorns) are the most commonly used form of pepper, the white peppercorns simply being the inner, fiery part of the berry with the dark, aromatic husk removed.

Oil
Most recipes call simply for oil. In these instances I have used groundnut oil, which I have found to be the best alternative to olive oil for everyday cooking. Where olive oil is specified, this is usually because its flavour is vital to that particular dish—for example, salads.

Bouquet Garni
This is a selection of aromatic herbs and spices tied together either with string or in a square of muslin. They can be bought ready made, but it is a delightful pastime to make up your own bouquet garni with herbs and flavourings tailor-made for each individual dish.

Chillies
These definitely require careful handling as the volatile oils readily make your eyes smart and your skin burn. Wear rubber gloves if possible. Cut the pods in half and sluice out the seeds under cold running water. Slice very finely with a sharp knife. After handling (even with gloves), wash your hands and chopping board thoroughly with plenty of soapy warm water to make sure no traces of the chillies linger.

Yoghurt
A lot of yoghurt is used in this book. If you use it in any quantity it is well worth investing in a yoghurt maker: follow the maker's instructions carefully and experiment with your own flavourings. For a really rich, round-flavoured yoghurt, try reducing the milk by gentle boiling (I use a milk saver in the base of the pan to prevent it from boiling over). Cool to about blood heat before using.

Flours
There are a wide variety on the market now and their names can be bewildering.

18

Wholemeal or wheatmeal flour. This contains all the wheat-grain (100%) including the bran and wheatgerm. It is coarser than other flours and its nutritional value higher. Go for the stoneground variety for a slightly longer shelf life. This is the flour most widely used throughout the book and is available in most supermarkets and shops.

81% or 85% extraction flours. These are usually sold as wheatmeal. This finer flour is obtained by sieving out the coarser bits, mostly the bran. Again, I recommend that you buy the stoneground variety with the extraction rate given on the packet.

Strong flour. This is of a 70–72% extraction rate, made from a hard wheat that has a high gluten content—and this is what you need for a good, light loaf. The gluten absorbs liquid, giving the flour the ability to stretch and expand in a way ordinary plain flour could never manage. With this degree of extraction, it stands to reason that there is very little bran or wheatgerm left in strong flour; to add insult to injury, the more widely-available brand names are bleached products. I refuse to subscribe to this madness and search out the un-bleached varieties of strong flour. Since the unbleached varieties of strong flours like wholewheat, granary, rye, barley, etc., have good flavour but little gluten, the best use of strong flour is in conjunction with these other flours to obtain a good, reasonably light and tasty bread.

SOUPS

People these days seem reluctant to make their own soups, but for the life of me I cannot think why.

Some authorities would have us believe that the public still strongly associates soup with pauperism, thanks to the charity soup kitchens which started back in the late eighteenth century. Cookery books of around that period do tend to come up with rather daunting titles like, 'A Nutritious Soup for the Laborious Poor', but I think this can be only part of the trouble. What is really wrong is people's over-exposure to the manufactured product—which is always entirely uniform, completely consistent and, for me, gutless. As for the latest type of 'soup' that you sprinkle into a cup and add boiling water: words fail me.

By now you will gather that I am something of a soup crusader and a glance at the following chapter will endorse this. I must admit that once I got going on these soup recipes I found it very hard to stop. They are worth a little extra time and effort because the reward lies in the home-made product being so much better and more varied than anything you can ever hope to find in those miserable packets and cans. The bedrock of a good soup is the stock and the best stock is home-made: it contributes a roundness and fullness of flavour that is simply unobtainable any other way. But I realise that to expect everyone to make their own stock is a counsel of perfection nowadays. The better-quality stock cubes available in the shops are acceptable but I would advise you to use these at slightly less strength than the manufacturer suggests. This allows the flavour of the other ingredients to come to the fore and not be obliterated by the all-pervading stock-cube flavour. Should you find that the finished soup lacks a little excitement, then bolster the flavour by the careful addition of mushroom ketchup, tomato paste, Worcestershire sauce, soy, etc.

Soup eaters usually fall into one of two categories, some finding it a meal in itself and others eating it only under sufferance as 'weak wash fit only for babes and invalids'. All I can say is, let the latter category have a go at some of these soups, because I am quite definitely in the soup-as-a-meal lobby. Hence most of these recipes can best be described as hearty family fare, which should be served in large portions accompanied only by good home-made bread, with cheeses and fresh fruit to follow.

Vegetable Bouillon

(Makes 1 generous litre/2 pints)

This recipe is highly adaptable. The bouillon can be used as stock for most of the soups in this chapter. If the soup you intend making is light-coloured, then skip browning the vegetables in fat beforehand and you will obtain a clearer, lighter-brown stock; the more robust soups will require the darker stock. The bouillon can also be served as a soup in its own right—either clear, or thickened with its own ingredients, sieved, and perhaps served with tiny wholemeal dumplings (page 32).

110 g (4 oz) haricot beans, or peelings from 1·25 kg (3 lb) well-scrubbed potatoes
1 huge Spanish onion
2 carrots
1 celery stalk
1 turnip (small apple size)
10 g (½ oz) butter
¼ teaspoon dried thyme
1 large bayleaf
1 tablespoon parsley stalks
2 cloves garlic
2·75 litres (5 pints) water
Salt and freshly ground black pepper

If you are not much of a potato-eating family and opt for using haricot beans, put them in a saucepan with 570 ml (1 pint) of water. Bring to the boil, simmer for 2 minutes, then leave aside, covered and away from the heat for about an hour.

Please note that it is not necessary to peel any of the vegetables. Simply trim the onion top and bottom and slough off any damaged or discoloured outside skin. Leave the inner orange-coloured skin intact, as it will add colour to the stock. Trim the carrots, celery and turnip, top and bottom and scrub well. Cut all the vegetables in 1 cm (½ in) slices.

24

Heat the butter in a large saucepan. When melted, stir the vegetables in thoroughly to coat with the butter. Leave to cook on a heat just below moderate for 15 minutes, stirring frequently so that the vegetables brown evenly and do not burn. After 15 minutes the vegetables and the base of the pan should have a good brown coating.

If you are using haricot beans, pour them and their soaking liquor into the pan and top up with the remaining 2·5 litres (4 pints) of cold water. Otherwise, stir in the potato peelings and pour in the full 2·75 litres (5 pints) of cold water. Throw in the herbs and the unpeeled whole garlic cloves. Bring to simmering point and simmer very gently uncovered for 3 hours.

Strain the contents of the stock pot into a large sieve set over a bowl. There should be 1 generous litre (2 pints) of liquid left. If it is less, make up to the quantity with fresh water. If more, boil the bouillon to reduce it. Season lightly and use as required.

Simple Chicken Stock   (*Makes 1 litre/2 pints*)

For speed, this stock is made in a pressure cooker and it is very much along the lines of recipes given in their accompanying handbooks. But, a word of warning. Do not be fooled into thinking that the longer you pressure-cook a stock the better it will be. In my experience the pressure cooking can go too far and rather strange, bone-tasting flavours develop; so stick to the cooking time given. If for some reason a strongly flavoured stock is needed, then release the pressure, uncover and continue cooking until it reaches the required strength. If you have no pressure cooker, simply put all the ingredients into a large saucepan with an extra 570 ml (1 pint) water and simmer, partially covered, for 1–1½ hours.

Carcass of a roast chicken
1 large onion or, for milder flavoured delicate soups, 1 large leek
2 celery stalks

2 carrots
A handful of parsley stalks
1 bayleaf
A pinch of thyme
½ teaspoon black peppercorns

Break the carcass into pieces and put into the pressure cooker. Trim the onion top and base, slough off the outer skin only, slice thickly and add. If you are using a leek instead, trim top and bottom, slice in half lengthways and wash thoroughly in between the leaves under cold running water. Slice across thickly and add to the pot. Trim the celery stalks and carrots top and bottom, scrub well, chunk and add, with the herbs, peppercorns and a generous litre (2 pints) of water. Cover, bring up to pressure and cook at 15 lb pressure for 15 minutes. Cool slowly, strain and store the stock, covered, in a cold place. Any fat can be skimmed off once it has solidified on the surface.

Note: A good, simple soup can be made from the stock above if any meat left on the carcass is returned to the strained stock and boiled up again with a good handful of crushed vermicelli and a few frozen peas for colour. Add any seasoning as required in the recipe.

Chilled Cucumber, Yoghurt and Buttermilk Soup

(Serves 6)

A good, well-flavoured yoghurt is all important in this recipe, so I always make my own: 1 generous litre (2 pints) of Channel Island milk boiled gently until reduced to about 845 ml (1½ pints) and then used to make the yoghurt. Try serving this soup well chilled with warm wheatmeal soda bread (see page 226), missing out the herbs but adding a level tablespoon of cummin seeds to the mix instead. Or turn the recipe into a good appetiser dip by missing out the buttermilk and adding more cucumber.

720 ml (1¼ pints) yoghurt
150 ml (¼ pint) buttermilk
1 large cucumber
2–3 teaspoons mint, finely chopped
1 teaspoon sea salt
½ teaspoon black peppercorns
Seeds from 1 cardamom pod
½ small clove garlic
2–3 teaspoons lemon juice
About 1 tablespoon olive oil
A little milk

Pour the yoghurt and buttermilk into a large bowl and beat together until smooth.

Trim the ends from the cucumber then coarsely grate the rest of it, unpeeled, directly into the bowl. Stir in the chopped mint (be careful: it should in no way be obtrusive).

Combine and crush the sea salt, peppercorns, cardamom seeds and garlic in a mortar, and stir into the soup. Cover and chill until ready to serve. Just before serving, beat in the lemon juice and oil, taste, and season carefully if required. Thin down the consistency with a little milk if you prefer. Serve each portion with an ice cube in it.

Spanish Iced Salad Soup   (*Serves 5–6*)

Like most foreign imports, this recipe has undergone all sorts of permutations never heard or even dreamt of in its mother country. Of course, there is no such thing as a definitive recipe, but this one combines all the essential elements (as far as I have been able to establish) and certainly is to my taste.

½ cucumber
4 spring onions
½ green pepper
8 black olives
450 g (1 lb) tomatoes
1 fat clove garlic, crushed
50 g (2 oz) wholemeal bread
3 tablespoons olive oil
1 tablespoon wine vinegar
A little lemon juice
Salt and freshly ground black pepper
A little tomato paste

Wipe and coarsely grate the cucumber. Trim the spring onions and finely chop; de-seed and very finely dice the green pepper; pit and finely chop the olives. Chop the tomatoes coarsely and and rub through a nylon sieve into a bowl. Stir in the grated cucumber and any juices, the pepper, olives and crushed garlic. Chill while preparing other ingredients.

Pour 150 ml (¼ pint) of cold water into a measuring jug and make up to 275 ml (½ pint) with ice cubes. Pour into a liquidiser goblet and add the wholemeal bread, olive oil and vinegar. Blend until the ice cubes have been broken down and incorporated into the mixture, then stir into the bowl. Taste, adding lemon juice, salt and freshly ground pepper as required. If you feel the soup lacks a bit of body, stir in a little tomato paste. Chill until ready to serve. Just before serving, coarsely crush some ice cubes and stir into the soup.

Note: A variety of garnishes can be served with the soup, such as finely diced cucumber and pepper, sliced radishes or spring onions, chopped olives, etc. Finely chopped hard-boiled eggs and tiny, crispy, fried croûtons are also good. Serve them all separately in small bowls so that people can help themselves.

Beetroot Soup (Hot or Chilled) (*Serves 6–8*)

Alas, this is one recipe where it *is* necessary to peel a vegetable. (Beetroots can end up with a very musty flavour when boiled in their skins.) If served hot, the soup can be made more substantial by cooking diced potatoes and shredded cabbage in it. It is this ability to fit the bill for everything, from a lovely starter for a summer dinner party to a hearty lunch on a cold winter's day, that makes this soup one of my all-time favourites.

700 g (1½ lb) young, raw beetroot
10 finger-thick spring onions
1·5 litres (2½ pints) chicken stock
A sprig of thyme
A few parsley stalks
¼ teaspoon dried dill weed
1 clove garlic, peeled and halved
1 cucumber
About 1 tablespoon wine vinegar
About 1 tablespoon lemon juice
Salt and freshly ground black pepper
Cream or soured cream, to serve
Chives, to garnish

Peel the beetroot and dice. Trim the spring onions, top and bottom, and chop. Put the beetroot and onions in a large saucepan with the stock, herbs and garlic. Bring to the boil and simmer uncovered for about 1 hour. By this time some of the colour will have gone from the beetroot to the surrounding liquid, leaving the beetroot a pinkish colour. Wash, trim and dice the cucumber. Add to the soup and continue to cook for a further 15 minutes.

If you wish to serve the soup chilled, simply allow the contents of the pan to drain through a sieve into a bowl. If it is to be served hot, rub the contents of the pan through a sieve or mouli and return the purée to the rinsed-out pan to reheat. Both versions should be flavoured with vinegar and lemon juice and some salt and freshly ground black pepper. Serve either well chilled with a marbling of cream or hot with soured cream, and sprinkled with snipped chives.

Spinach and Buttermilk Soup with Prawns
(Serves 6)

Like most green soups this tends to lose its beautiful fresh colour fairly quickly, but it is none the worse for that. If using prawns, try to buy fresh ones and peel them yourself. (Freeze debris and use as a basis for a fish stock.) However, since prawns are an expensive luxury, you can leave them out, if you wish, and the result will still be a delicious soup.

700 g (1½ lb) spinach
25 g (1 oz) butter
1 tablespoon chopped spring onions
425 ml (¾ pint) buttermilk
About 150 ml (¼ pint) vegetable stock
Juice ½ large lemon
1 teaspoon chopped fresh tarragon
110 g (4 oz) peeled prawns
2 tablespoons medium sherry
Salt and freshly ground black pepper
Thinned soured cream, to serve

Wash the spinach well in plenty of cold water. Remove and discard the stalks and any damaged leaves, and transfer the rest to a colander to drain thoroughly.

Heat the butter in a large saucepan. Stir in the spring onions and cook gently in the butter for a couple of minutes before turning the heat up high and adding the spinach. Keep the spinach constantly on the move until all the leaves have wilted and most of the moisture has evaporated. Transfer to the goblet of a liquidiser, add the buttermilk and blend briefly until the spinach is chopped down to approximately tea-leaf size. Pour into a bowl and stir in the vegetable stock, lemon juice and tarragon.

Finely chop the prawns and add half to the soup. Add the sherry and salt and freshly ground black pepper to taste. Thin the soup with a little additional stock if necessary then chill before serving. Serve each portion with a blob of thinned soured cream, topped with a sprinkling of the reserved chopped prawns.

Puréed Vegetable Soup with Wholewheat Spätzle

(*Serves 6–8*)

Spätzle ('Little Sparrows') are a German dish. They are small soup dumplings made, in this case, with a simple wholewheat-flour batter mixture. They come out about the size and shape of peeled shrimps (probably where the 'Little Sparrows' part comes in).

1 generous litre (2 pints) browned vegetable bouillon (see page 24)
1 tablespoon tomato paste
Dash of soy sauce
Generous squeeze of lemon juice
Salt and freshly ground black pepper
Yoghurt, to serve

Spätzle:
175 g (6 oz) wholewheat flour
½ teaspoon salt
Freshly grated nutmeg
2 eggs
About 100 ml (4 fl oz) milk

Through a sieve or mouli, rub enough of the vegetables into the strained bouillon to form a thin soup. Pour the purée into a saucepan and re-heat, tasting and adding the flavouring ingredients as required.

While the soup heats, make the *Spätzle*. Put the flour, salt and nutmeg into a bowl and make a well in the centre. Break in the eggs and beat with a wooden spoon, gradually incorporating the flour and milk in stages until a smooth batter is formed. Add enough milk so that a spoonful of mixture scooped out of the bowl is just thick enough to hold itself on the spoon.

Once the soup is simmering, position a colander over the top and put a spoonful of batter mix into the base. Use a flat-based rubber or plastic spatula to push the batter through the colander holes: it will drop into the soup to form little dumplings. As you complete each batch, give the soup a stir before continuing with the next. After the last batch, simmer for 2 minutes before serving piping hot, with yoghurt.

White Dairy Soup   (*Serves 6*)

I admit that I am normally put off by white soup, but this one is rather special. A delicious soup, in fact, with a slightly lactic flavour: very velvety and warming.

1 medium onion
2 whites of leek
40 g (1½ oz) butter
25 g (1 oz) flour
570 ml (1 pint) chicken stock
570 ml (1 pint) milk
150 ml (¼ pint) yoghurt
175 g (6 oz) curd cheese
2 eggs
Salt and freshly ground white pepper
Chopped watercress or chives, to garnish

Trim all the green parts and root from the leeks. Slice in half lengthways then across into pieces ½ cm (¼ in) thick. Wash thoroughly in cold water and drain in a colander. Peel and chop the onion.

In a large pan heat the butter until frothy. Add the drained leeks and chopped onion and stir well to coat the vegetables with butter. Cover and cook gently for 10 minutes until softened but not coloured. Uncover, sprinkle in the flour, and stir to mix thoroughly before gradually adding the stock and milk. Bring to simmering point, stirring frequently, then cook gently, uncovered, for a further 10 minutes.

Liquidise the contents of the pan and return the purée to the rinsed-out pan, off the heat.

Now, without bothering to rinse out the liquidiser goblet, put in the yoghurt, curd cheese and eggs and blend until smooth. Stir this into the warm soup and heat gently, still stirring. Bring the soup up to a serveable temperature, but no more (if it boils it will curdle). Taste and season with salt and freshly ground white pepper. Serve garnished with chopped watercress or chives.

Note: If you are not using a liquidiser simply rub the soup through a sieve or mouli and, in a bowl, combine the curd cheese gradually with the yoghurt before mixing in the lightly beaten eggs.

Chestnut and Celeriac Soup   (*Serves 5–6*)

The task of peeling chestnuts can cause a break-up in the happiest of homes, but the fact remains that there is no easy way around this. Tinned whole chestnuts, or debris, are simply not the same. And neither, unfortunately, are the nice-looking dried chestnuts (shelled, of course) which are occasionally obtainable in Spanish or Italian shops in this country. I thought I had found the answer when I came across these but the results were disappointing. Bribery and absolutely equal division of labour are the only way to keep the peace. On your own it will take 35 minutes to peel 450 g (1 lb) of chestnuts!

450 g (1 lb) chestnuts
Salt and freshly ground black pepper
About 700 g (1½ lb) celeriac roots
1 white of leek
2 slices streaky bacon
50 g (2 oz) butter
1 generous litre (2 pints) strong chicken stock
Bouquet garni of 1 bayleaf, generous pinch of thyme and a
    few crushed parsley stalks
Chopped watercress leaves, to garnish

Nick the ends of the chestnuts with a small, sharp knife and simmer in boiling, salted water for 10 minutes. Taking out about 4 chestnuts at a time peel the shells and inner skins, before removing the next batch, otherwise they will cool off or dry out and become difficult to peel.

Thickly peel the celeriac roots and dice. Rind and chop the bacon. Trim and chop the leek.

Melt the butter in a large pan. When frothy, stir in the bacon. When the fat begins to run, stir in the diced celeriac and chopped leek. Quarter the chestnuts into the pan and stir, to coat with butter. Cook over a moderate heat, stirring frequently for 10 minutes or until a nice brown crust forms on the base of the pan. Pour in the stock, and bring to simmering point, stirring. Add the bouquet garni, cover and simmer very gently for 10–15 minutes, until the chestnuts and celeriac in particular are just tender, not mushy. Squeeze and discard the bouquet garni. Briefly liquidise the contents of the pan, so that there are some identifiable lumpy bits left in the soup.

Return the soup to the pan and thin to the desired consistency with water. It will probably need about 425–570 ml ($\frac{3}{4}$–1 pint) of water. Re-heat, taste and season with salt and freshly milled black pepper. Serve piping hot, garnished with chopped watercress.

Watercress and Potato Soup   (*Serves 5-6*)

These two main ingredients may seem strange bedfellows but there is a simple strategy to make this recipe work: half the watercress is used to establish a background flavour; the other half is chopped and stirred in at the last moment, thereby retaining that lovely, fresh, slightly peppery watercress taste.

700 g (1½ lb) old potatoes
2 medium Spanish onions
2 bunches watercress
50 g (2 oz) butter
570 ml (1 pint) chicken stock
570 ml (1 pint) full cream milk
Squeeze of lemon juice
Salt and freshly ground black pepper

Peel and cut the potatoes in chunks. Peel and chop the onions. Wash the watercress in cold water and drain on kitchen paper. Pick over carefully, discarding the thick stalks and any damaged leaves. Chop *half* the leaves only. Put the rest aside.

Melt the butter in a large saucepan. As soon as it is frothy, stir in the chopped onions and potatoes. Cook over a low heat, stirring occasionally, for about 10 minutes or until the onions are softened but not coloured. Pour in the stock and milk and sprinkle in the chopped watercress leaves. Bring to the boil, then turn the heat down and leave the soup to simmer very gently, uncovered, for 20–25 minutes or until the vegetables are absolutely tender.

Pour the contents of the pan into the goblet of the liquidiser and blend until smooth. (You will probably need to carry out this stage in several batches.) Return the purée to the rinsed-out pan and re-heat. Now chop the remaining watercress and add it to the soup. Taste and flavour, using a generous squeeze of lemon juice, some salt and freshly ground black pepper. Serve piping hot.

Mushroom and Barley Soup   (*Serves 4–5*)

For the majority of people, the only mushrooms available are the nondescript white button variety which really do not have much flavour and are best eaten raw. If you have any choice in the matter at all, buy open or flat mushrooms for cooking. If, on the other hand, you are fortunate enough to be able to buy—better still pick—field mushrooms then so much the better, as they will make a good soup even more delicious.

1 generous litre (2 pints) chicken stock
50 g (2 oz) pearl barley
1 clove garlic, crushed
Pinch each of dried sage, oregano and rosemary
1 onion
225 g (8 oz) mushrooms
25 g (1 oz) butter
Juice of ½ a small lemon
Salt and freshly ground black pepper

Heat the stock in a saucepan. When the liquid boils, trickle the barley into it in a thin stream through your fingers. Add the crushed garlic and the herbs, then cover and simmer gently for 1 hour or until the barley is tender.

Peel and very finely chop the onion. Wipe the mushrooms with a piece of damp kitchen paper, then chop them very finely.

Heat the butter in a medium pan, allowing it to froth until lightly brown before stirring in the onions. Cook gently for 10 minutes before turning the heat up high and stirring in the chopped mushrooms. Stir and cook for 1 minute before pouring in the stock and barley. Add the lemon juice, taste and season with salt and a liberal amount of freshly ground black pepper. Bring to the boil and simmer gently for 2 or 3 minutes. Serve piping hot.

Butter Bean and Bacon Soup (*Serves 5–6*)

225 g (8 oz) butter beans
1 bayleaf
110 g (4 oz) slices streaky bacon
1 large onion
2 smallish celery stalks
25 g (1 oz) butter
2 tablespoons oil
About 150 ml (¼ pint) creamy milk
Salt and freshly ground black pepper
Chopped parsley, to garnish

Put the butter beans in a medium saucepan with a generous litre (2 pints) of water and bring to the boil. Boil for 1 minute, turn off the heat under the pan, cover and leave aside for 1 hour. Add the bayleaf and any bacon rinds you might have to the pan and bring to the boil once more. Cover and simmer gently for 45 minutes.

Meanwhile, peel and finely chop the onion, scrub and finely chop the celery (leaves as well if any are attached). Heat the butter and oil in a large saucepan and stir in the prepared vegetables. While these are cooking gently, chop the bacon and add to the pan. Cook for about 10 minutes so that the ingredients are softened but not coloured.

When the beans have had their 45 minutes, tip them and their cooking liquor into the large pan, cover and continue cooking gently for a further 15 minutes or until all the beans and vegetables are soft. Discard the bacon rinds.

Now draw the pan off the heat and, armed with a potato masher, simply squash the beans down to a soft pulpiness. Thin with milk and re-heat. Taste and season with salt and freshly ground black pepper and serve hot, garnished with chopped parsley.

Yoghurt is good with most types of vegetable soup and this is no exception.

Chick Pea and Tomato Soup   (*Serves 5–6*)

Whole chick peas are just a little too chunky to manage decorously on a soup spoon, so the cook had to effect a compromise: half liquidised, half mashed!

225 g (8 oz) chick peas, soaked overnight in 1 scant litre
  (1½ pints) water
1 large onion
3 tablespoons oil
2 cloves garlic, crushed
1 teaspoon dried oregano
2 tablespoons tomato paste
275 ml (½ pint) strong chicken stock
396 g (14 oz) tin tomatoes
Dash of tabasco
Salt and freshly ground black pepper
Yoghurt, to serve

Pour the chick peas and their soaking water into a medium saucepan. Bring to the boil, then cover and simmer for 45 minutes to 1 hour, or until the chick peas are soft. Do not add any salt until later in the recipe. Drain the peas and measure the cooking liquor; make up to a scant litre (1½ pints) with fresh water if necessary.

Peel and chop the onion. In a large saucepan heat the oil and gently fry the onion until golden and softened. Stir in the crushed garlic, oregano and tomato paste. Add the chicken stock and the contents of the tin of tomatoes. Return the chick peas and their liquor to the pan and stir to break down the tomatoes. Liquidise half the soup and, using a potato masher, mash down the remaining half to break up the peas. Mix the two halves together again and re-heat. Taste and season with tabasco, salt and freshly ground black pepper. Serve piping hot with a spoonful of yoghurt stirred into each portion.

Spicy Lentil Soup   (*Serves* 5–6)

This soup has a certain amount of 'heat' in it already (the chilli) but if on tasting the finished soup you think it could do with still more, then adjust to your taste by adding tabasco, a drop or two at a time. If fresh chillies are unavailable use a dried chilli, de-seeded and crumbled.

1 large onion
1 potato
1 green chilli
10 g (½ oz) butter
1 tablespoon oil
1 scant litre (1½ pints) chicken stock
396 g (14 oz) tin tomatoes
175 g (6 oz) brown lentils
4 cardamom pods
1 scant teaspoon caraway seeds
Generous squeeze of lemon juice
Salt and freshly ground black pepper
Yoghurt, to serve

Peel and chop the onion and scrub and dice the potato. Cut the stalk end off the chilli and slit lengthways. Sluice away the seeds inside under cold running water, drain and chop fairly finely.

Heat the butter and oil in a large saucepan. Stir in the chopped onion, potato and chilli and fry until lightly browned. Pour in the chicken stock and the contents of the tin of tomatoes. Make sure you pick the lentils over carefully before rinsing them in a sieve and adding to the pan. Crush the cardamom pods and take out the little black seeds. Discard the pods and add the seeds to the soup. Bring the soup to boiling point, then cover and simmer gently for 45 minutes, or until the lentils are soft (test them by eating some).

Transfer the contents of the pan to a liquidiser and blend briefly: just long enough to leave interesting bits in it, without reducing the lot to a uniform purée. Return the soup to the pan and sprinkle in the caraway seeds. Re-heat and consider the consistency. If you intend to eat the soup as a main meal, then it can stand being thicker than if it is intended as a starter. Thin with additional stock or water, then taste and flavour with lemon juice, salt and freshly ground black pepper.

Serve piping hot with a heaped teaspoon of yoghurt in each portion.

Pea Pod Soup (*Serves 4–5*)

This recipe came about because it has always hurt me to throw away pea pods. Since it also uses up one or two other bits and bobs that might have been destined for the bin, I admit to a real *bonne femme* feeling of satisfaction when I watch people enjoy this soup.

The pods from 900 g (2 lb) young peas
The green tops from a bunch of spring onions
175 g (6 oz) coarse, outside leaves of lettuce
A sprig of savory
1 generous litre (2 pints) chicken stock
1 egg yolk
150 ml (¼ pint) single cream
Squeeze of lemon juice
Salt and freshly ground black pepper
Snipped chives, to garnish

Pile the pea pods in a colander and sluice with cold water. Drain and put into a large pan. Whisk the spring onion tops and lettuce leaves around in a bowl of cold water, drain, chop coarsely and put in the pan with the savory. Pour in the stock and bring to the boil. Simmer gently, uncovered, for about 20 minutes or until the pea pods in particular are soft.

Set a large sieve over a bowl and rub the contents of the pan through the sieve. There will be a fair amount of stringy fibre left which you discard. Return the purée to the rinsed-out pan and re-heat.

In a separate bowl, beat the egg yolk and cream together. Gradually pour this into the soup in a thin stream, whisking quickly as you do so (use a balloon whisk for this if possible). Continue to heat, stirring until the soup has slightly thickened and is the consistency of thin cream. Do not let the soup boil once the egg yolk has been added. Taste and flavour with the lemon juice and some salt and freshly ground black pepper. Serve hot, sprinkled with the chopped chives.

Minestrone (*Serves 5–6*)

This has got to be the 'grand-daddy' of all vegetable soups. If you look carefully enough, you may even find a kitchen sink in the list of ingredients! My only requirement for this soup is that you can stand a spoon up in it—and with this recipe you will certainly be able to do so. Different seasons will require different vegetables to be substituted, but steer clear of strong root vegetables and stick to leeks and potatoes, etc.

225 g (8 oz) red kidney or haricot beans
1 large onion
2 carrots
2 celery stalks
3 courgettes
½ small head of cabbage
225 g (8 oz) green beans
4 tomatoes
110 g (4 oz) fat bacon slices
4–5 tablespoons olive oil
1 fat clove garlic, crushed
1 teaspoon dried, or 1 tablespoon fresh, chopped basil
50 g (2 oz) brown rice
110 g (4 oz) fresh peas
2 tablespoons freshly chopped parlsey
Salt and freshly ground black pepper

Put the beans in a saucepan with 1 generous litre (2 pints) of cold water. Bring to the boil, boil for 2 minutes, then remove from the heat. Cover and leave aside for 1 hour, then bring to the boil and simmer, covered, for 1 hour or until the beans are tender.

Meanwhile, prepare the vegetables. Peel and dice the onion. Scrub and top and tail the carrots, celery stalks and courgettes. Dice the carrots and celery; slice the courgettes into four lengthways then across into 1 cm (½ in) pieces; cut the beans into similar lengths. Quarter, core and shred the cabbage; peel and coarsely chop the tomatoes. Finally, rind and dice the bacon.

Select your largest cooking pot, heat 3 tablespoons oil in it

44

and gently fry the onion, carrots, celery and bacon for about 10 minutes. Pour in 1·75 litres (3 pints) of water, bring to the boil and add the courgettes, beans, cabbage, crushed garlic, basil and rinsed rice. Pour in the cooked beans and their liquor, bring to simmering point and simmer gently for 35 minutes. Add the tomatoes and peas and simmer for a further 15 minutes or until everything is tender. Sprinkle with parsley and pour in the balance of fresh olive oil. Taste and season with salt and freshly ground black pepper.

Serve piping hot in large bowls with plenty of Parmesan cheese and some hunks of fresh, wholemeal bread.

SALADS

Dismiss all thoughts of rabbit food from your mind! Or, if you cannot cope with that degree of mental gymnastics, a quick thumb through the next few pages should change your ideas. As you will see, salad does not necessarily equal lettuce. In fact in only one of the recipes is this true. These are mostly main-meal salads, real tuck-in-and-enjoy ones that would fill even a Canadian lumberjack!

There is still a place, though, for the simple green salad. Sometimes a few crisp lettuce leaves and a couple of thinly sliced mushrooms tossed in the simplest of salad dressings fits the bill in a way no other form of vegetable could. But just as the making of a very simple, classic dress requires considerable skill, so too with a basic salad (and many other 'simple' dishes, come to that!). Your ingredients need to be spanking fresh and crisp because there will be no flavour, garnish or sauce for them to hide behind.

Wash lettuce leaves only as a last resort. It is generally possible to avoid this with the inner leaves and try to get away with merely wiping outer ones with a piece of damp kitchen paper. If necessary, dry thoroughly, again using kitchen paper, or spin them in a clean tea towel out of doors. (My eccentric mother actually uses her spin dryer for this purpose: I'm sure that's a selling angle no washing-machine manufacturer has ever dreamt of!) Discard all leaves but those in A1 condition and tear up the larger ones, keeping the smaller ones whole. If the leaves are then spread out on a tea towel, rolled up loosely and stowed away in the lowest part of a refrigerator they will keep happily until serving time, provided it is the same day.

Salad dressings are very much a personal thing. Flavour with garlic, fresh herbs or flavoured vinegars if you like, but I suggest a basic ratio of 6 parts olive oil to 1 of wine vinegar. *Olive* oil, please! And when I say that oils vary considerably in flavour from those that are so bland they seem starched and laundered to those with a good ripe fruity flavour, you can

48

judge where my tastes lie! Vinegar should be herb flavoured, sherry, cider or wine, but never, never malt! Put the vinegar (or lemon juice), English or French mustard, crushed salt and black peppercorns in a screw-topped jar with any other flavourings you choose. Shake vigorously until the salt dissolves. Spoon in the oil and shake again until the mixture forms an emulsion.

Have the crisp, dry salad leaves lightly chilled in a large bowl and, when ready to serve, spoon about 2 tablespoons of the dressing over the leaves and toss them in the dressing with your hands. This makes sure that no puddles of dressing accumulate in the bottom of the salad bowl and the leaves remain crisp and unbruised after being tossed. Serve immediately, handing the remaining dressing around separately in a jug.

Beet and Apple Salad with Walnuts

(Serves 5–6)

A good winter salad. I have also served this as a main-course salad, with the addition of salted herring which has been soaked, cut into strips and forked into the salad just before serving.

1 small head of celery
About 350 g (12 oz) cooked beetroot
2 tart eating apples
1 head chicory
50 g (2 oz) walnut pieces
1 teaspoon chives, snipped

Mustard Vinaigrette:
3 tablespoons Dijon mustard
3 tablespoons wine vinegar
150 ml ($\frac{1}{4}$ pint) olive oil
About 1 tablespoon lemon juice
1 tablespoon parsley, chopped
Salt and freshly ground black pepper

To garnish:
2 hard-boiled eggs
1 tablespoon parsley, chopped
1 head chicory

Trim and finely dice the celery, reserving the celery leaves. Dice the peeled beetroot and apples (leaving the skins on). Remove a conical core from the base of the head of chicory, then slice it into four lengthways, before slicing fairly thinly across. Chop the walnut pieces and combine with the chives and the rest of the prepared vegetables in a large bowl. Chill until ready to serve.

Just before serving, combine all the ingredients for the mustard vinaigrette in a bowl and whisk together with a fork until thoroughly mixed. Make sure the dressing is seasoned well before pouring over the vegetables and tossing everything together. Break the remaining head of chicory down into the single spears and stick upright against the edge of the bowl around the salad. Rub the hard-boiled eggs through a nylon sieve on to the salad and, finally, chop the reserved celery leaves and sprinkle the salad with these and the parsley.

Cracked Wheat Salad (*Serves* 6)

If you have never eaten cracked wheat (sometimes called bulghur), imagine nutty-tasting, damp breadcrumbs. Flavoured with loads of parsley, mint and lemon juice, it really becomes something very different and delicious—one of my favourite salads in fact. Bulghur can be bought from health food shops, or Greek or Middle Eastern food stores.

225 g (8 oz) fine cracked wheat
6 spring onions, with plenty of green tops
25 g (1 oz) fresh mint leaves
3 heaped tablespoons freshly and finely chopped parsley
3 tablespoons olive oil
3 tablespoons lemon juice
Salt and freshly ground black pepper

Garnish:
Black olives, sliced
Tomatoes, sliced
Cucumber, sliced
Fresh sprig of mint

Soak the cracked wheat in a large bowl, covered with plenty of cold water, for about 45 minutes or until the wheat is soft when nibbled.

Line a colander with a clean tea towel and tip in the contents of the bowl. Gather up the ends of the towel and squeeze as much moisture out of the grains as you can. Then spread the towel out and leave the grains to dry for about 30 minutes.

Meanwhile trim the onions top and bottom and finely chop with the fresh mint. Transfer the cracked wheat to a bowl and fork in the chopped onions, mint and parsley, then add the oil, lemon juice and salt and freshly ground black pepper to taste.

Pile the salad up on a large serving plate and garnish with sliced olives, tomatoes, cucumber and sprig of mint.

Three Bean Salad   (*Serves 6*)

In case anyone has not yet got the message, do not add any salt to the peas and beans until they are cooked as this really seems to slow down the softening process. The red kidney beans have to be boiled separately as they give off a fair amount of their colour during cooking.

110 g (4 oz) chick peas
110 g (4 oz) white kidney beans } soaked separately overnight
110 g (4 oz) red kidney beans
1 Spanish onion
1 large green pepper
1 fresh chilli

Dressing:
6 tablespoons olive oil
1 tablespoon white wine vinegar
1 tablespoon lemon juice
1 clove garlic, crushed
2 rounded tablespoons parsley, chopped
Salt and freshly ground black pepper

Garnish:
2 tomatoes, thinly sliced
6–8 black olives

Drain the chick peas and put in a saucepan with plenty of fresh water to cover. Bring to the boil, cover and cook gently for 1 hour. Uncover and add the drained white beans (and some additional boiling water if necessary, to cover generously) then re-cover and continue to simmer for a further 45–60 minutes. As soon as the white beans are tender, remove the pan from the heat. While the chick peas and white beans cook, boil the red kidney beans separately, in the same way, for about 45 minutes.

Meanwhile, peel and dice the onion: halve, de-seed and dice the pepper. Halve the chilli lengthways, rinse out the seeds and slice very thinly.

To prepare the dressing, simply combine all the ingredients together in a large bowl. Drain the cooked peas and beans thoroughly, then add immediately to the bowl and turn them carefully in the dressing. Cool a little before forking in the onion, pepper and chilli, then cover and chill lightly until ready to serve. Taste and season well with salt and freshly ground black pepper. Arrange the thinly sliced tomatoes around the edge and the pitted olives in the centre.

Caesar Salad   *Serves 5–6)*

This is an American classic, some of whose followers have devoted their lives to making their version of the the most perfect Caesar Salad. The rules are simple: chill the lettuce *and* the salad bowl, then make the salad and eat it immediately!

2 cos lettuces
2 fat cloves garlic
150 ml ($\frac{1}{4}$ pint) olive oil
4 slices wholemeal bread, $\frac{1}{2}$ cm ($\frac{1}{4}$ in) thick
3–4 tablespoons vegetable oil
2 standard (No. 4) eggs, at room temperature
Salt and freshly ground black pepper
4 tablespoons lemon juice
6 tablespoons freshly grated Parmesan
6 chopped anchovy fillets

Separate the lettuce leaves, wiping the outer ones with a piece of damp kitchen paper. Break the leaves up into roughly 5 cm (2 in) lengths and roll up loosely in a clean, damp tea towel. Store at the bottom of the refrigerator with a very large salad bowl, allowing ample time for both to chill *thoroughly.*

Peel and crush, but do not mash, the garlic cloves. Leave in the measured olive oil for at least one hour to flavour it adequately.

Trim off the crusts and cut the bread into $\frac{1}{2}$-cm ($\frac{1}{4}$ in) dice. Heat the vegetable oil in a pan and fry the cubes of bread, turning them constantly, until they rustle crisply against the side of the pan. Drain on kitchen paper until ready to serve.

53

You can use raw eggs for this salad but, if your system rebels at the thought, plunge the eggs into boiling water for *60 seconds only*. Remove and leave to cool.

With everyone seated at the table, transfer the lettuce to the bowl. Season with salt and freshly ground black pepper and strain in the olive oil. Using your hands, lightly toss the leaves until they are thoroughly coated. Break in the raw (or coddled) eggs, add the lemon juice and toss again, as lightly but as thoroughly as you can manage. Sprinkle in the cheese, and add the anchovy fillets and croûtons. Toss once more and serve.

Note: You may like to try what the Americans call a Western Salad. This may be more popular with the younger members of the family and is simply the above recipe with crumbled Blue cheese substituted for the anchovies.

Brown Lentil and Mushroom Salad
(Serves 4–5)

225 g (8 oz) brown lentils
1 small onion
1 clove garlic
1 bayleaf
½ teaspoon dried thyme
225 g (8 oz) cup mushrooms
1 strip of lemon zest
Juice of 1 lemon
3 tablespoons parsley, chopped
Salt and freshly ground black pepper
4 slices streaky bacon
Additional chopped parsley, to garnish

Dressing:
½ Spanish onion
6 tablespoons olive oil
2 tablespoons wine vinegar
1 teaspoon Dijon mustard
1 teaspoon crushed coriander seeds

Pick the lentils over carefully, discarding any small stones, sticks, etc. Rinse in a sieve and transfer to a saucepan. Peel, quarter and add the onion to the pan with the whole garlic clove, bayleaf and thyme. Add enough cold water to cover the lentils by about 2·5 cm (1 in), bring to the boil, cover and simmer for 15–30 minutes, until the lentils are tender but not mushy.

Meanwhile, finely dice the Spanish onion and combine with the olive oil, vinegar, mustard and coriander seeds in a bowl. Wipe the mushrooms over and cut each one into six wedges.

As soon as the lentils are cooked, drain and reserve the cooking liquor. Stir the lentils into the dressing in the bowl. Make the reserved liquor up to about 425 ml (¾ pint) with fresh water and return to the pan with a strip of lemon zest and half the lemon juice. Bring to the boil and add the mushrooms. When the liquid returns to the boil remove the pan from the heat, drain the mushrooms and add them to the lentils with the remaining lemon juice and the parsley. Taste and season with salt and freshly ground black pepper.

Rind and grill the bacon until absolutely crisp, cool and crumble over the top of the salad. Chill lightly and serve garnished with a little additional chopped parsley.

Chick Pea Dip Salad (*Serves 6–8*)

This is a salad made up of puréed chick peas, mixed with fried onion and pine nuts and covered with a minty yoghurt dressing. It can be served either as a starter on its own with crispbread or pitta, or as a dip using a selection of fresh salad vegetables to scoop it up. Another idea is to serve it as a main-course salad. I usually present it on a large oval meat platter surrounded by sticks of carrots, cucumber, celery, spring onions, pieces of cauliflower, radishes, chicory spears, raw mushrooms, etc. Any way, it is rather delicious.

225 g (8 oz) chick peas, soaked overnight
½ teaspoon dried oregano
1 onion, finely chopped
25 g (1 oz) butter
50 g (2 oz) pine nuts
2 tablespoons parsley, finely chopped
1 clove garlic, crushed
Juice of 1 lemon
Tabasco
About 4 tablespoons olive oil
Salt and freshly ground black pepper

Yoghurt Topping:
150 ml (¼ pint) yoghurt
Generous squeeze lemon juice
1 clove garlic, crushed
2 rounded tablespoons chopped mint
2 tablespoons sesame seeds

56

Drain the soaked chick peas and cook for 1–2 hours with the oregano in plenty of fresh, boiling, unsalted water until tender. Drain, reserving the cooking liquor.

Either liquidise the drained chick peas with about 200 ml (7 fl oz) of their cooking liquor or mash well and then add the liquid.

Melt the butter in the same pan (don't bother to wash it) and fry the finely chopped onion and pine nuts until the pine nuts are golden. Stir this into the chick pea mixture with the chopped parsley and crushed garlic. Add the lemon juice and season with salt and freshly ground black pepper. Lastly, add sufficient tabasco for your taste and enough olive oil to give the mixture a 'dip-able' consistency. Spread on a serving dish.

In a bowl, combine the yoghurt, lemon juice, crushed garlic and mint and whisk until smooth. Taste and season with salt and freshly ground black pepper. Pour this over the chick pea mixture and sprinkle with the toasted sesame seeds. Chill until ready to serve.

Aduki Bean and Brown Rice Salad
(Serves 4–6)

The boiling and rinsing of the aduki beans may appear a little unnecessary, but in practice they produce a cloudy, coloured water which needs to be discarded before the rice can be boiled with the beans. Always go easy with the monosodium glutamate: usually you need only one or two short shakes of it!

110 g (4 oz) aduki beans, soaked overnight
1 large mug brown rice
2 mugs boiling chicken stock, or water
2 small green peppers
2 celery stalks
½ cucumber
2 small green chillies

Dressing:
110 ml (4 fl oz) olive oil
1 tablespoon lemon juice
1 fat clove garlic, crushed
Plenty of freshly ground black pepper
1 teaspoon sea salt, crushed
2 tablespoons parsley, finely chopped
2 tablespoons celery leaves, finely chopped
Dash of monosodium glutamate

Put the beans and their soaking water in a pan, bring to the boil and cook for one minute; cover and leave aside for 1 hour. Now boil them for 15 minutes, then drain and sluice with cold water. Return them to the pan, add the rinsed and drained rice and pour in the boiling stock or water. Bring to boiling point, cover and simmer very gently for about 40 minutes. Uncover and see if all the liquid has been absorbed. If the beans and rice are cooked (they should keep just a little 'bite'), cook uncovered until no free liquid remains. If they still seem a little undercooked for your taste, continue cooking them covered until ready.

While the beans and rice are cooking, combine the dressing ingredients in a large bowl. Tip the rice and bean mixture into the bowl, turn lightly with a fork and leave until cold.

De-seed and dice the peppers; scrub and finely slice the celery stalks and dice the cucumber. Trim the stalk ends from the chillies, slice lengthways and rinse away the seeds; finely chop the chillies. Fork all the prepared vegetables into the cooled rice and bean mixture and taste; you may find it needs a little extra lemon juice, salt or pepper.

Chinese-Style Chicken Salad (*Serves 4–5*)

Much easier than it sounds!

1 small red pepper
1 small green pepper
15 cm (6 in) piece cucumber
½ bunch watercress
225 g (8 oz) fresh beansprouts
175 g (6 oz) cooked chicken meat

Dressing:
1 small onion
1 small celery stalk
2·5 cm (1 in) piece fresh ginger, peeled
75 ml (3 fl oz) groundnut oil or sesame-seed oil
55 ml (2 fl oz) white wine vinegar
2 tablespoons light soy sauce
2 teaspoons tomato paste
2 teaspoons lemon juice
Salt and freshly ground black pepper

Seed and dice the peppers; dice the cucumber. Rinse, dry and select only the leaves and tender stalks of watercress. Briefly rinse the beansprouts in cold water and dry thoroughly on kitchen paper. Cut the chicken meat into slivers. Combine all these ingredients in a serving bowl, cover with cling film and chill lightly until ready to serve.

For the dressing, peel and thickly slice the onion, scrub and roughly chop the celery. Combine these and the remaining dressing ingredients in the goblet of a liquidiser, add 55 ml (2 fl oz) of cold water and blend until smooth. Taste and season as required. Chill lightly before serving separately with the salad so that people can help themselves.

Pearl Barley Salad *(Serves 5–6)*

I usually serve this around April or May when I'm longing for salads but the ingredients are still rather expensive in the shops. The recipe makes the most of what is available and is an unusual and successful way of serving pearl barley.

½ cucumber
4–6 finger-thick spring onions
About 20 radishes
175 g (6 oz) pearl barley
3 tablespoons parsley, chopped
110 ml (4 fl oz) olive oil
3 tablespoons lemon juice
1 clove garlic, crushed

Garnish:
2–3 tomatoes, sliced
cucumber, sliced
½ red or green pepper, finely chopped

Start by dicing the cucumber, putting it in a colander and sprinkling with a teaspoon of salt. Leave to drain while preparing the rest of the salad. Trim the spring onions stem and stern and slice thinly. Slice the radishes the same way.

Rinse the pearl barley in a sieve under cold, running water. Transfer to a saucepan containing about 2½ litres (4 pints) of boiling salted water. Boil uncovered for 30 minutes, then drain in a sieve and sluice with cold water. Transfer the barley to a colander, place over a pan of simmering water and cover the barley with a clean, folded tea towel. Wedge a saucepan lid down on top and steam in this manner for a further 30 minutes. By this time the barley should be tender and dry.

While the barley is cooking, prepare the dressing by combining the olive oil, lemon juice and garlic in a mixing bowl. Add the hot, cooked barley, fork through to combine thoroughly with the dressing and leave to cool. Add the prepared spring onions, radishes and chopped parsley. Rinse the cucumber briefly with cold water, dry on kitchen paper and add to the salad. Toss well, taste and season with salt and freshly ground black pepper. Chill, until ready to serve.

Serve the salad piled up on a flat plate. Garnish the edge of the plate with cucumber slices, the edge of the salad with sliced tomatoes and the centre with finely chopped pepper.

Curried Wholewheat Macaroni Salad
(*Serves 5–6*)

This is a delicious and rather different salad, a meal in its own right requiring only some salad greens like lettuce or chicory and some fresh wholemeal bread to be served with it.

225 g (8 oz) wholewheat short-cut macaroni
10 radishes
2 stalks celery
2 carrots
1 green pepper
½ cucumber
6 finger-thick spring onions
Salt and freshly ground black pepper

Curry Dressing:
150 ml (¼ pint) home-made mayonnaise
1 tablespoon hot curry powder
1 tablespoon wine vinegar
2 tablespoons yoghurt
2 tablespoons home-made chutney

Boil the macaroni in salted water until just tender. While the pasta is cooking, combine the mayonnaise, curry powder, wine vinegar, yoghurt and chutney in a large bowl. As soon as the pasta is cooked, drain it thoroughly in a colander, then transfer to the bowl and turn in the curry sauce. Cover and leave aside while preparing the vegetables.

Top, tail and rinse the radishes in cold water and slice thinly. Scrub the celery stalks, slice in half lengthways then across fairly thinly, to form neat pieces. Top, tail and scrub the

61

carrots, then coarsely grate on to a plate. Halve, de-seed and dice the pepper; dice the cucumber. Lastly trim the spring onions, top and bottom, then slice across thinly. Stir the prepared vegetables into the cooled pasta, taste, and season with salt and some freshly ground black pepper if you think it needs it. Chill lightly before serving.

Mushroom Salad with Cider Dressing
(Serves 4 or 6)

This is a cooked mushroom salad that can be served either as a starter for 6 people with a chicory or watercress garnish, or as an accompaniment for 4 to cold meats with jacket potatoes and home-made pickles.

450 g (1 lb) button mushrooms
150 ml (¼ pint) dry cider
1 teaspoon coriander seeds

Dressing:
6 black olives
1 small onion
1 tablespoon cider vinegar
1 teaspoon coarse salt
½ teaspoon brown sugar
1 teaspoon French mustard
150 ml (¼ pint) olive oil
1 tablespoon parsley, chopped
Salt and freshly ground black pepper

Wipe the mushrooms with damp kitchen paper and trim the stems almost level with the caps.

Put the prepared mushrooms in a saucepan with the cider. Crush the coriander seeds and add to the pan. Cook uncovered until the cider has all but evaporated, giving the mushrooms a gentle stir occasionally so that they are evenly cooked. This will take about 10 minutes.

While they are are cooking, prepare the dressing by first

pitting and coarsely chopping the olives and peeling and finely dicing the onion. Measure the vinegar into a bowl then gradually whisk in the remaining ingredients one after the other in the order they appear in the list above. Stir in the prepared olives, onion and parsley, taste and season carefully.

Pour the dressing on to the hot mushrooms in the pan and leave to cool before covering and chilling in the refrigerator until ready to serve.

Chick Pea Salad with Blue Cheese Dressing *(Serves 4–6)*

I am very fond of zingy salads, and of this one in particular. It is not as savage as it sounds!

225 g (8 oz) chick peas, soaked overnight
Bouquet garni
2 hard-boiled eggs
110 g (4 oz) button mushrooms
6 spring onions, with plenty of green tops
1 large green pepper
½ teaspoon black peppercorns
1 teaspoon rock salt
50 g (2 oz) streaky bacon slices

Dressing:
6 tablespoons olive oil
1 tablespoon white wine vinegar
1 tablespoon lemon juice
2 tablespoons thick cream or mayonnaise
50 g (2 oz) Blue cheese

Drain the soaked chick peas and cook with the bouquet garni in plenty of fresh, boiling, unsalted water until tender. This will take anything from 1–2 hours. Drain, discarding the bouquet garni.

Meanwhile, peel and chop the hard-boiled eggs. Wipe, trim and cut each mushroom into six or eight sections, depending on size. Trim the onions at top and bottom and

63

finely slice. Wipe, halve and de-seed the pepper, then cut it into six wedges.

To make the dressing, simply combine all the ingredients in the goblet of a liquidiser with a heaped tablespoon of the drained chick peas. Blend until smooth and pour over the rest of the peas. Add the prepared mushrooms but not quite all of the chopped egg and spring onion—these will be used later as a garnish.

Crush the rock salt and peppercorns and add to the salad.

Arrange the wedges of pepper, skin-side-up on a grill rack with the bacon. Grill the bacon until crisp and reserve. Carry on cooking the pepper until the skin is absolutely black, then peel off the blackened skin and dice the flesh. Add the pepper to the salad, stir, taste and season again if necessary. Sprinkle the reserved egg and onion over the surface and finally the crumbled bacon. Cover and chill until ready to serve.

Brown Rice, Lentil and Mushroom Salad
(Serves 6)

1 mug brown rice
Salt
1 mug brown lentils
110 g (4 oz) button mushrooms
8 spring onions, with green tops
1 large green pepper
15 cm (6 in) piece cucumber
1 ripe avocado
Juice of 1 lemon

Dressing:
6 tablespoons olive oil
1 tablespoon wine vinegar
1 teaspoon French mustard
1 clove garlic, crushed
Freshly ground black pepper

Garnish:
2 heaped tablespoons parsley, chopped
2 tomatoes, thinly sliced

Put the rice in a pan, add 2 mugs of boiling water and some salt. Bring to simmering point, cover and cook gently for 40–45 minutes or until the rice is just tender and all the liquid is absorbed.

In a separate pan cook the lentils in plenty of boiling water for about 30 minutes, until tender but not mushy.

Meanwhile, prepare the dressing by combining the oil, vinegar, mustard, crushed garlic, salt and freshly ground black pepper in a bowl. Drain the cooked lentils and add with the cooked rice to the dressing and leave to cool.

Wipe the mushrooms over with a piece of damp kitchen paper and trim the stalks. Slice the caps thinly. Top and tail the spring onions, then slice thinly. Halve, de-seed and dice the pepper; dice the cucumber. Fold these vegetables into the lentil and rice mixture, cover and chill lightly until ready to serve.

Just before serving, halve, pit, peel and dice the avocado flesh. Lightly toss in the lemon juice and add to the salad. Toss again and taste and season well.

Heap the salad up on a serving dish, garnish with chopped parsley and surround with thin slices of tomato.

PIZZAS AND PIES

In the last few years pizzas and pies, mainly in the form of quiches or flans, have become immensely popular—and small wonder, for they are wonderfully versatile and convenient. A quiche will fit the bill from the grandest dinner party to an impromptu picnic and pizzas can be adapted to fit most tastes, pockets and occasions. As you read through the recipes, you will see that I have come up with a few rather different variations on the old themes.

Since I started to make pastry with brown flours, a whole new variety and combination of flavours has opened up to me. The nuttiness of wholewheat flour marries up extremely well with all sorts of flavours in a way that the orthodox white-flour pastry could never hope to do. It blends well with, and boosts the flavours of, such diverse foods as lactic cheeses and smoked fish. Also, if you have never thought of doing a brown-bread base for a pizza, do try it: I have used a very quick, one-rise technique that works beautifully.

But there is one problem with this section. I know that many people have a lot of trouble with pastry. For the most part, I have suggested a basic shortcrust using a combination of plain and self-raising wholewheat flours. This seems to give just that vital lift to what can sometimes be a frankly 'wangy' pastry! I have also added just slightly more water than is usual with a normal shortcrust, as this makes a more manageable dough and minimises the brown sawdust-type consistency which many people decry in short wholewheat pastry.

The lining of the flan tin, too, is a useful technique to get under your culinary belt. And, please note, flan *tins*, not oven glass plates or French porcelain, no matter how pretty! Tin ware allows pastry to cook through quickly and thoroughly in a way glass or porcelain never will.

Leek and Curd Cheese Flan   (*Serves 6*)

Pastry case:
75 g (3 oz) wholewheat flour
75 g (3 oz) self-raising 81% farmhouse flour
40 g (1½ oz) butter
40 g (1½ oz) lard

Filling:
8 thumb-thick leeks weighing a generous 450 g (1 lb)
25 g (1 oz) butter
110 g (4 oz) curd cheese
2 eggs
150 ml (¼ pint) milk
2 tablespoons yoghurt
A little nutmeg, freshly grated
Salt and freshly ground black pepper
40 g (1½ oz) stale Cheddar cheese

Pre-heat the oven to 190 °C (375 °F/mark 5)

Put a baking sheet to heat in the oven while you prepare the pastry.

Combine the flours together in a bowl, add the fats and rub in until the mixture resembles fine breadcrumbs. Stir in just enough water to combine to a stiff dough. Roll out on a floured surface and use to line a greased 24–25·5 cm (9½–10 in) flan tin with a removable base. Prick the base with a fork, and transfer to the baking sheet in the oven and bake for 20 minutes. Cool the flan case a little, leaving the baking sheet in the oven. Reduce the oven heat to 180 °C (350 ° F/mark 4).

Meanwhile, trim the leeks and slice in half lengthways. Cut across into pieces about ½ cm (¼ in) thick. Rinse well in cold water and drain in a colander.

Heat the butter in a medium saucepan. Stir in the prepared leeks and cook, uncovered, over a fairly high heat, stirring occasionally until all the excess liquid has evaporated from the pan and the leeks are softened. Remove the pan from the heat, crumble in the curd cheese and leave to soften and melt for 2 or 3 minutes in the residual heat of the pan. Break the eggs into

69

a bowl and lightly beat together with the milk and yoghurt. Gradually stir this into the pan. Taste and add nutmeg, salt and freshly ground black pepper and spoon the filling into the flan case. Quickly grate the Cheddar cheese over the flan and return to the oven to cook on the baking sheet for 30 minutes or until the filling is slightly puffed and golden. Serve hot or cold.

Fresh Herb Quiche (*Serves* 6)

The balance of herbs you use in this recipe is important but impossible to specify since it depends on what is available. Obviously, play down the strong ones such as sage, thyme, rosemary and mint, but go to town on the gentler ones like marjoram, basil, lovage, etc. The amount of sorrel you use will affect the amount of lemon juice needed to spike up the flavour —I usually use only a couple of leaves to the teaspoon of lemon juice required.

Pastry case:
See Leek and Curd Cheese Flan (page 69)

Filling:
6 finger-thick spring onions with as much green top as
  possible
10 g (½ oz) butter
3 rounded tablespoons chopped herbs (sage, thyme, mint,
  tarragon, basil, rosemary, majoram, lovage, sorrel, etc.)
1 bunch watercress leaves, leaves only
2 large (No. 2) eggs
150 ml (¼ pt) milk
150 ml (¼ pt) single cream
1 teaspoon sea salt
½ teaspoon black peppercorns
1 small clove garlic
Grated rind of ½ lemon
About 1 teaspoon lemon juice

Pre-heat the oven to 190 °C (375 °F/mark 5)

Follow the instructions for the making, lining and baking of the pastry flan case as in Leek and Curd Cheese Flan (page 69). Remove the baked flan case from the oven and put aside to cool, leaving the baking sheet in the oven. Reduce the oven temperature to 180 °C (350 °F/mark 4).

Meanwhile, prepare the filling. Trim the spring onions at top and bottom then finely chop. Heat the butter in a small saucepan and gently fry the onions for 5 minutes while you rinse, dry and finely chop the other green herbs and watercress leaves.

Combine the eggs, milk and cream together in a bowl and whisk lightly. Stir in the onions and any buttery juices from the saucepan and add the chopped herbs. Crush the sea salt, peppercorns and garlic together in a pestle and mortar and whisk into the mixture with the lemon rind. Taste and add salt, freshly ground black pepper and lemon juice as necessary. Leave the herb mixture aside for about an hour so that the flavours can develop, then pour the filling into the prepared flan case.

Bake on a pre-heated baking sheet at 180 °C (350 °F/mark 4) for 35–40 minutes, until the mixture is slightly puffed all over. Serve warm or cold. (You will be disappointed if you serve the quiche hot, as the herb flavours do not come through.) Lovely eaten with a yoghurty-dressed salad and excellent summer picnic fare.

out effective combination of flavours. The yoghurt
d to counter-balance the sweetness of the carrots.

e:

and Curd Cheese Flan (page 69), but add
on marjoram to pastry mix

lb) carrots
) butter
tablespoons parsley, chopped
lic, crushed
150 ml (pint) milk
150 ml (¼ pint) yoghurt
3 eggs
Freshly grated nutmeg
Salt and freshly ground black pepper

Pre-heat the oven to 190 °C (375 °F/mark 5)

Follow instructions for the making, lining and baking of the
pastry flan case as in Leek and Curd Cheese Flan (page 69).
Remove the baked flan case from the oven and put aside to cool,
leaving the baking sheet in the oven. Reduce oven temperature
to 180 °C (350 °F/mark 4).

While the flan is baking prepare the filling. Trim and
quarter the leeks lengthways. Cut into ½ cm (¼ in) slices, wash
thoroughly in cold water and drain. Top, tail and scrub the
carrots, then grate coarsely on to a plate.

Melt the butter in a medium pan. When frothy, stir in the
leeks. As soon as they have softened, add the grated carrots.
Cook over a moderate heat, stirring frequently, until all the
moisture has evaporated from the vegetables and the carrots
are just starting to stick to the base of the pan. Remove from
the heat and stir in the parsley and garlic.

In a bowl whisk together the milk, yoghurt and eggs. Stir
this into the carrot mixture and season well, adding salt and
freshly ground black pepper and nutmeg to taste. Spread into

the slightly cooled pastry case and return to the oven to bake
on the baking sheet for about 45 minutes or until the filling is
set in the centre. Serve hot with additional yoghurt.

Blue Cheese and Spring Onion Quiche (*Serves* 6)

There is quite a zingy flavour to this quiche. It is rather rich
—using 275 ml (½ pint) of single cream—but you could use half
milk half cream if the budget will not stretch to all cream.

Pastry case:
See Leek and Curd Cheese Flan (page 69)

Filling:
4–6 spring onions, with plenty of green tops
110 g (4 oz) Blue cheese
110 g (4 oz) curd cheese
3 eggs
275 ml (½ pint) single cream
2 tablespoons parsley, chopped
Salt and freshly ground black pepper

Pre-heat the oven to 190 °C (375 °F/mark 5)

Follow the instructions for making, lining and baking of the
pastry flan case as in Leek and Curd Cheese Flan (page 69).
Remove the baked flan case from the oven and put aside to
cool, leaving the baking sheet in the oven. Reduce oven
temperature to 180 °C (350 °F/mark 4).
   Prepare the filling while the flan is baking. Trim the onions
top and bottom then finely chop.
   Put the two cheeses in a bowl and mash together either with
a fork or an electric hand whisk. Gradually beat in the eggs,
one by one, followed by the cream and mix until the mixture is
comparatively smooth (a few pieces of cheese here and there
are nothing to worry about). Stir in the chopped onion and
half the parsley. Taste and season with salt and freshly ground

74

black pepper. Pour into the cooled flan case and return to the oven to bake on the baking sheet. Just before closing the door, scatter the remaining tablespoon of parsley over the surface. Bake for 35 minutes or until lightly puffed and golden. Serve hot, warm or cold.

Watercress Quiche   (*Serves* 6)

Close your eyes and you could almost be eating asparagus when you taste this flan. The marriage of wholewheat pastry and filling is especially good in this recipe.

Pastry case:
See Leek and Curd Cheese Flan (page 69)

Filling:
2 bunches watercress
1 onion
10 g (½ oz) butter
50 g (2 oz) Wensleydale cheese
3 eggs
275 ml (½ pint) milk
150 ml (¼ pint) single cream
1 teaspoon mustard powder
Salt and freshly ground black pepper

Pre-heat the oven to 190 °C (375 °F/mark 5)

Follow instructions for the making, lining and baking of the pastry flan case as in Leek and Curd Cheese Flan (page 69). Remove the baked flan case from the oven and put aside to cool, leaving the baking sheet in the oven. Reduce oven temperature to 180 °C (350 °F/mark 4).

Prepare the filling while the pastry is baking. Wash, dry and remove the leaves from the watercress, discarding the stalks. Finely chop the leaves. Peel and finely chop the onion.

Heat the butter in a small saucepan. Stir in and gently cook the onion for about 10 minutes, until softened. Spread the onion on to the base of the flan case and then grate the cheese on top.

Break the eggs into a bowl and whisk in the milk, cream, mustard powder, salt and freshly ground black pepper. Stir in the chopped watercress. Pour the majority of the filling into the flan case and return to the oven to sit on the baking sheet before adding the remainder. Bake for about 35 minutes or until slightly puffed and golden.

Kidney Bean and Brown Rice Flan

(Serves 6)

Filling:
110 g (4 oz) brown rice
75 g (3 oz) red kidney beans
2 onions
25 g (1 oz) butter
2 eggs
225 ml (8 fl oz) milk
75 g (3 oz) strong Cheddar cheese, grated
1 teaspoon dried tarragon
1 teaspoon Worcestershire sauce
1 teaspoon salt
Freshly ground black pepper

Pastry case:
See Leek and Curd Cheese Flan (page 69)

Pre-heat the oven to 190 °C (375 °F/mark 5)

First of all rinse the rice and beans separately, then cook separately in salted boiling water until tender—both will take about 35–40 minutes. The reason they are boiled separately is that sometimes a good deal of colour seems to come out of the beans as they cook and this would tint the rice a rather extraordinary shade.

Meanwhile, make, line and bake a pastry flan case as outlined in the recipe for Leek and Curd Cheese Flan (page 69). When baked, remove the flan case from the oven and set aside to cool, leaving the baking sheet in the oven. Reduce the oven temperature to 180 °C (350 °F/mark 4).

Prepare the rest of the filling by peeling and finely chopping the onions. Gently fry them in the butter until softened and golden and remove the pan from the heat.

Beat the eggs and milk together in a bowl. Add the thoroughly cooked and drained rice and kidney beans, the fried onions, grated cheese and remaining filling ingredients. Mix thoroughly, taste and season well with salt and freshly ground black pepper. Pour the filling into the slightly cooled flan case and return to the oven to bake on the baking sheet for

35–40 minutes or until the edge of the filling is beginning to brown. Serve hot or warm.

Potato and Cheese Flan   (*Serves 6*)

The recipe calls for four cooked potatoes but if you do not have this many left over from a meal, simply boil the scrubbed potatoes in their skins until just tender. Leave them to cool then slice and use, skins as well.

Pastry case:
See Leek and Curd Cheese Flan (page 69)

Filling:
6 spring onions with plenty of green tops
4 medium cooked cold potatoes
50 g (2 oz) grated Parmesan cheese
Salt and freshly ground black pepper
Freshly grated nutmeg
3 eggs
275 ml (½ pint) milk
3 tablespoons flour
½ teaspoon dried thyme
25 g (1 oz) butter

Pre-heat the oven to 190 °C (375 °F/mark 5)

Follow instructions for making, lining and baking of the pastry case as in Leek and Curd Cheese Flan (page 69). Remove the baked flan case from the oven and put aside to cool, leaving the baking sheet in the oven.

Trim the spring onions and finely slice. Cut the cold potatoes into ½ cm (¼ in) thick slices (skins and all if you like).

Sprinkle a third of the sliced onions in the base of the cooled pastry case. Arrange half the cold, sliced potatoes on top, sprinkle with half the Parmesan, another third of spring onions, then some salt, pepper and a little grated nutmeg. Cover with the remaining potato slices, spring onions and, finally, Parmesan cheese.

In a bowl whisk together the eggs, milk, flour and thyme. Taste and season then pour carefully over the flan. Dot the top with butter and bake at 190 °C (375 °F/mark 5) for 45–50 minutes or until the potato topping is golden and crispy. Serve warm or cold with a crisp green salad and yoghurt dressing.

Quick Frying-Pan Pizza   (*Serves 4*)

This is what I class as a desperation recipe. Of course it's a cheat but extreme situations call for desperate remedies. You can have this pizza on the table within 15 minutes flat and from a standing start at that! If you can coerce someone into rushing together a coleslaw while you attend to the pizza, it should halt the most ravenous hordes in their path.

225 g (8 oz) 81% self-raising flour
½ teaspoon salt
Freshly ground black pepper
4–5 tablespoons olive oil
4 generous tablespoons tomato paste
397 g (14 oz) tin tomatoes
About 150 g (5 oz) St Paulin or Port Salut cheese
1 dozen black olives, pitted and chopped
1 teaspoon mixed herbs
50 g (1¾ oz) tin anchovies in oil

Combine the flour, salt and some freshly ground black pepper in a bowl. Make a well in the centre and spoon in 2 tablespoons of olive oil, followed by 4 tablespoons of water. Stir to form a soft, but not sticky, dough; it may need 1–1½ tablespoons more water to come together. Turn the dough out on to a floured surface and knead lightly. Roll out to a round big enough to fit into the base of a 23–25·5 cm (9–10 in) frying pan.

Heat a good tablespoon of olive oil in the frying pan. Lay the dough round in the pan and cook over a low heat for 5 minutes. By this time the base should be nicely browned. Invert the pan on to a large plate. Heat a further tablespoon of olive oil in the pan before returning the dough to the pan to cook the other side for 5 minutes.

While it cooks spread the top, browned, surface with tomato paste. Drain and roughly chop the tomatoes, then spread over the surface of the dough. I do not for one moment expect you to discard the tinned tomato juice—this can be used up in a thousand ways in cooking! Dice the cheese and sprinkle over with the chopped olives and herbs. Lastly, drape the anchovy fillets round and about the top and drizzle the oil from the tin over the pizza.

When the underside is browned, cook the surface of the pizza under the grill for 2 or 3 minutes to melt the cheese and thoroughly heat through the topping. Serve immediately.

Note: Unlike the orthodox pizza, which tends to be a bit chewy, this is just as good served cold.

Pissaladière

A good, cheap recipe if you are practically skint. To spin it out to its maximum, put the pizza in a large swiss roll tin, 33 × 23 cm (13 × 9 in). If you prefer a thicker base and filling, use a small swiss-roll tin 28 × 18 cm (11 × 7 in).

Filling:
900 g (2 lb) large onions
About 4 tablespoons olive oil
1 fat clove garlic
Salt and freshly ground black pepper
56 g (2 oz) tin anchovy fillets in oil
About 1 dozen black olives, halved and pitted
½ teaspoon dried mixed herbs

Bread base:
225 g (8 oz) wholewheat flour
1 teaspoon salt
1 teaspoon dried mixed herbs
Freshly ground black pepper
175 ml (6 fl oz) hand-hot water
1 teaspoon sugar
1 teaspoon dried yeast

Start by preparing the filling because this needs about 40 minutes to cook.

Peel and thinly slice the onions. Heat 3 tablespoons of olive oil in a large saucepan and stir in the onions. Peel, chop and crush the garlic with some salt and add to the pan. Cook over a low heat for 35–40 minutes, stirring occasionally, until the onions have just about formed a soft mass and started sticking to the base of the pan. Remove from the heat and leave to cool.

Meanwhile, combine the flour, salt, herbs and some freshly ground black pepper together in a bowl.

Pour 150 ml (¼ pint) of hand-hot water into a separate bowl and use a fork to whisk in the sugar, followed by the yeast. Leave aside for 10 minutes to froth. Pour this on to the flour mixture and add a further 25 ml (1 fl oz) of hand-hot water and stir to form a dough. Scoop out the dough on to a floured surface and roll out to roughly the size of the baking tin being used. Oil the baking tin and put the bread base in, pushing up the sides and into the corners with your fingers. Brush with olive oil, cover with a clean cloth and leave to rise in a warm place for 20 to 30 minutes.

Pre-heat the oven to 220 °C (425 °F/mark 7).

Spread the cooled onion filling over the bread base. Drain and reserve the oil from the tin of anchovies. Slice the fillets lengthways and arrange in a lattice-work pattern over the onion filling. Stud each diamond with a halved, pitted olive. Sprinkle with the herbs and drizzle the reserved anchovy oil over the whole pizza.

Bake in the pre-heated oven for 20 minutes. To make sure the bread base is cooked underneath in the centre, lift up the edge of the pizza and take a look. Serve with a tomato salad and coleslaw.

Pizza Al Tonno (*Serves 5–6*)

This pizza can be made into a 25·5–28 cm (10–11 in) round or to fit a small swiss-roll tin, size 28 × 18 cm (11 × 7 in)—whichever your tins, or whims, dictate!

Filling:
198 g (7 oz) tin tuna in oil
1 onion
225 g (8 oz) tin tomatoes
1 bayleaf
½ teaspoon basil
¼ teaspoon marjoram
1 scant teaspoon sugar
Salt and freshly ground black pepper
56 g (2 oz) tin anchovy fillets in oil
About 1 dozen black olives, halved and pitted
2–3 tablespoons Parmesan cheese, grated

Bread base:
See Pissaladière (page 82)

Prepare the filling by first draining the oil from the tin of tuna into a medium saucepan. Peel and finely chop the onion and stir into the pan. Cook gently for about 10 minutes until softened and golden. Stir in the tuna, tomatoes, herbs and sugar and season with a little salt and freshly ground black pepper. Cook gently, uncovered, for about 20–25 minutes, stirring occasionally, until the sauce has cooked to a jam-like consistency. Remove the pan from the heat and leave to cool.

Meanwhile, prepare the bread base as for Pissaladière (page 82), forming the pizza into the size you have chosen. Brush with oil, cover with a clean cloth and leave in a warm place to rise for 20–30 minutes.

Pre-heat the oven to 220 °C (425 °F/mark 7).

Discard the bayleaf and spread the cooked filling over the base to within about 1 cm ($\frac{1}{2}$ in) of the edge.

Drain the anchovy fillets, reserving the oil, halve lengthways and arrange them in a lattice pattern on top and stud each diamond with a halved, pitted olive. Sprinkle with the Parmesan cheese and drizzle the reserved anchovy oil over the surface.

Bake for 20 minutes. Serve hot or cold.

Wholewheat Pizza with Ratatouille Topping

(*Serves 6*)

Ratatouille:
2 aubergines about 350 g (12 oz)
3 courgettes about 350 g (12 oz)
2 medium onions
1 large pepper
3–4 tablespoons oil
397 g (14 oz) tin tomatoes
1 teaspoon dried basil
2 cloves garlic, crushed
Salt and freshly ground black pepper

Bread base:
See Pissaladière (page 82)

Topping:
Olive oil
110 g (4 oz) Mozzarella or Dutch Gouda cheese
50 g (1¾ oz) tin anchovy fillets
1 teaspoon mixed, dried herbs

Start by preparing the filling.

Wipe the aubergines, top and tail and cut into just under 1 cm (½ in) cubes. Top and tail the courgettes and quarter lengthways, then cut across into cubes. Dice the onion, de-seed and dice the pepper

Heat the oil in a large saucepan and gently fry the chopped onions until softened but not coloured. Add the drained contents of the tin of tomatoes, then the aubergines, courgettes and pepper, followed by the basil and crushed garlic and some salt and freshly ground black pepper. Cover and simmer gently for 15 minutes, then uncover and simmer for a further 15 minutes or until all the ingredients combine nicely to give a suitable sauce-like consistency for a topping. Remove the pan from the heat, taste and season again if necessary before leaving to cool.

Meanwhile, make up the bread base as for Pissaladière (page 82). Use to line a large swiss-roll tin. Brush with olive oil, cover with a cloth and leave to rise for about 30 minutes in a warm place.

Pre-heat the oven to 220 °C (425 °F/mark 7).

Spread the cooled filling over the bread base. Slice the cheese as thinly as possible and lay at random over the filling. Cut the anchovy fillets in half lengthways and use to form a lattice-work pattern on the surface of the pizza. Finally, sprinkle with the herbs and drizzle any anchovy oil left in the tin over the top.

Bake in the top half of the oven for about 25 minutes or until well browned and bubbling. Check to make sure the bread base is cooked by levering up the pizza with a fish slice or palette knife and taking a good look. Serve hot or cold.

Cheese and Vegetable Lattice Pie (*Serves 6*)

A good recipe for using up left-overs.

Pastry:
110 g (4 oz) plain flour
110 g (4 oz) wholewheat flour
½ teaspoon salt
Freshly ground black pepper
50 g (2 oz) butter
50 g (2 oz) lard
75 g (3 oz) stale Cheddar cheese

Filling:
2 leeks
450 g (1 lb) cooked vegetables (celery, carrot, turnips, parsnips, peppers, potatoes, etc.)
50 g (2 oz) butter
4 tablespoons flour
275 ml (½ pint) milk
175 g (6 oz) curd cheese
1 egg, lightly beaten
½ teaspoon dried marjoram
Squeeze of lemon juice
Salt and freshly ground black pepper

To make the pastry, combine the flours and seasoning together in a bowl. Rub in the fats until the mixture is like fine breadcrumbs. Grate the cheese and fork into the mixture. Add just sufficient cold water to combine everything to a stiff, but not sticky, dough. Cut off about one-third of the dough and reserve. Roll out the remaining dough fairly thickly, about $\frac{1}{2}$ cm ($\frac{1}{4}$ in) thick, and use to line a greased 20 × 4 cm (8 × 1$\frac{1}{2}$ in) sandwich tin. Trim away any surplus pastry around the edge and reserve.

Prepare the leeks for the filling by trimming top and bottom. Cut them in four lengthways, then across into 1 cm ($\frac{1}{2}$ in) thick slices. Wash thoroughly in a bowl of cold water and drain well in a colander. Dice the cooked vegetables. Melt the butter in a medium saucepan and stir in the drained leeks. Cover and cook gently for 10 minutes or until the leeks are just tender. Stir in the flour and cook for a minute or two before gradually adding the milk. Bring to the boil, stirring. Boil gently for a minute before removing the pan from the heat. Crumble the curd cheese and add to the sauce. Beat it in, and when it has melted add the lightly beaten egg and marjoram. Taste and flavour with the lemon juice and some salt and freshly ground black pepper. Fold in the vegetables and leave until cold, before spreading the mixture into the pastry-lined tin.

Pre-heat the oven to 200 °C (400 °F/mark 6).
Put a baking tray in the top half of the oven. Spread the cooled filling into the pastry-lined tin, then roll out the combined reserved pastry and trimmings and use to create a latticework effect on top of the pie. Place in the oven on the baking sheet, and bake for about 40 minutes or until golden brown. Serve hot or cold.

Egg, Curd Cheese and Herb Pie

(*Serves* 6)

A rather unusual, tasty pie, lovely for summer picnics.

Pastry:
110 g (4 oz) wholewheat flour
110 g (4 oz) self-raising 85% unbleached flour
110 g (4 oz) fat: ½ lard ½ butter
1 egg white, to glaze
2–3 teaspoons sesame seeds, to coat

Filling:
25 g (1 oz) mint leaves
150 ml (¼ pint) soured cream
110 g (4 oz) curd cheese
1 rounded tablespoon snipped chives
Salt and freshly ground black pepper
5 standard (No. 4) eggs
2 tablespoons Parmesan cheese, grated

Pre-heat the oven to 200 °C (400 °F/mark 6)

Make the pastry in the usual way, sieving the flours together into a bowl and rubbing in the fats until the mixture resembles breadcrumbs. Form the mixture into a stiff unsticky dough using cold water. Roll out two-thirds of the dough into a round and use to line a 23 cm (9 in) diameter 3 cm (1¼ in) deep, sloping-sided pie tin. Add any trimmings to the remaining third of pastry and reserve.

Rinse and dry the mint leaves on kitchen paper and chop finely.

In a bowl beat together the soured cream and curd cheese until smooth. Add the mint and chives and season to taste with salt and freshly ground black pepper. Spread a good half of the mixture evenly on the pastry-lined base of the pie tin. Break the five eggs over the surface and blob the remaining mix between the eggs so that it distributes them evenly in the pie. Sprinkle with the Parmesan cheese and a little additional salt and freshly ground black pepper. Dampen the rim of the pie with water. Roll out the remaining pastry and lay over the filling. Seal well, trim off any excess and decorate the edge, firmly crimping together between thumb and forefinger. Glaze the top of the pie with the lightly beaten egg white and sprinkle evenly with the sesame seeds.

Bake for 25 minutes or until nicely browned. At this stage, the eggs should be just creamily set—not dry, but not runny either. Serve warm or cold with a green salad and yoghurt.

Wholewheat Spinach and Nut Pasties   (*Makes 8*)

This is good portable food for lunch boxes and picnics. But bear in mind that the filling is wrapped in pastry: if you are eating it cold, you need to make sure that it has a pretty zingy flavour before you bake it.

Pastry:
175 g (6 oz) hard block margarine
110 g (4 oz) plain wholewheat flour
110 g (4 oz) 85% unbleached self-raising flour
Good pinch of salt
Beaten egg, to glaze
Sesame seeds, to coat

Filling:
700 g (1½ lb) fresh spinach
6 spring onions with green tops
75 g (3 oz) brazil nuts, shelled
175 g (6 oz) cottage cheese
50 g (2 oz) Parmesan cheese, grated
1 small clove garlic, crushed
Freshly grated nutmeg
1 oz (25 g) butter, melted
About 1 tablespoon lemon juice
Salt and freshly ground black pepper

Weigh the margarine, wrap in greaseproof paper and freeze for 30 minutes.

Meanwhile, combine the flours and salt in a bowl. When you take the margarine from the freezer, half unwrap it and, holding it by the paper, dip it in the flour, then coarsely grate directly into the bowl. Keep dipping the fat in the flour and toss the grated bits with a fork to keep them separate in the flour. When all the fat is grated, cut any lumps down into the mixture with a knife. Add sufficient cold water to form the mixture into a dough that leaves the side of the bowl clean. Chill the dough in a plastic bag while preparing the filling.

Wash the spinach in plenty of cold water, pick over carefully, discarding stalks and damaged leaves and transfer to a colander to drain. Top and tail the spring onions and chop finely. Chop the brazil nuts.

Put the spinach in a large saucepan and cook over a high heat, without additional water, turning the leaves constantly, until they are just wilted. Drain in a colander until cool enough to handle, then squeeze the spinach dry in your hands. Chop finely and transfer to a bowl. Add the onions, nuts, the cheeses and the rest of the flavouring ingredients, mix and moisten with the melted butter. Taste and season well with salt and freshly ground black pepper. The filling needs to have a really positive flavour.

Pre-heat the oven to 220 °C (425 °F/mark 7).

Roll out the pastry approximately 3 mm ($\frac{1}{8}$ in) thin. Using a saucepan lid or plate as a cutting guide, you should get eight 15 cm (6 in) rounds from this quantity, including the re-rolling of pastry scraps. Divide the filling into eight and place on one half of each pastry round. Brush the edges with beaten egg and bring the other halves over to enclose the filling and form the pasties. Seal the edges well and crimp attractively between thumb and forefinger. Brush the pasties with egg and dip in the sesame seeds. Bake on a greased baking sheet for 20–25 minutes or until nicely browned. Serve hot or cold.

PASTA AND RICE

Pasta, for all its current popularity, is still dreadfully misused and abused. In Soho trattorias I have been served with spaghetti strips fused together in a solid sheet like a matchstick raft! It should be a healthy, nourishing food, endlessly versatile and interesting, not a certain way of acquiring heartburn before the dessert. This unhappy state can be avoided by paying attention to the quality of the pasta and its cooking.

Ordinary pasta is made from finely-ground semolina, derived from a hard, durum wheat. This contains a fair amount of vitamins, proteins and minerals and so is a good base for any number of quick, simple dishes, excellent for family meals.

However, just lately there has appeared on the market a range of wholewheat pasta which I have tried and can thoroughly recommend. Most of the recipes in this chapter have been tested with the wholewheat kind or my own home-made version, which I think is best of all.

As soon as you start to cook pasta the term *al dente* will crop up and most people will know by now that it means 'to the tooth'. This is a description of the precise stage at which the pasta is cooked through and no more, when one should be able to bite a piece and still find it firm enough to offer a resistance to the teeth. Pasta needs boiling in plenty of salted water, about 4·6 litres (4 quarts) water to 450 g (1 lb) of pasta and 1½ heaped tablespoons of salt. Add the pasta all at once as soon as the water has come to a rapid boil. Stir to prevent it sticking together and keep tasting it to test how the cooking is progressing. The instant the pasta is cooked (and it is wisest to err on the side of *under* cooking), drain it immediately into a colander. Transfer to a warmed serving dish, add butter, seasoning and sauce, then toss and serve immediately so that the pasta remains hot and does not go to the table overcooked.

Rice should be tackled in much the same way as pasta. Almost without exception, the recipes call for *brown* rice—and I cheerfully admit to being hooked. I wouldn't give you tuppence for white and, to my mind, brown rice has the edge over it in almost every respect: texture, flavour and nutritional value.

You could argue, however, that it has one drawback and

this is the length of time it takes to cook: about double that of white rice, or 45–50 minutes. I usually measure the rice in a large mug and use the same one to measure the water or stock, which should be 2–2½ times the amount of rice used. Brown rice is best eaten chewy but if you prefer it a little more tender you will need an extra ½ mug of stock to carry on the cooking. The best method is one which allows the rice to cook without being stirred, so cook the measured amount in 2½ times its volume of liquid, in a covered pan over a gentle heat. When it has had 40 minutes, have a look and a taste. If it is cooked, remove the lid and evaporate any remaining excess liquid by boiling fast. If it is still too chewy, then add a little more liquid to help it on its way. Once cooked, pull the pan off the heat, put a folded tea towel over the top and jam the saucepan lid back on. The rice can be kept warm like this for about 30 minutes and come to no harm. If you cook with gas and have gas pilot lights, the minimum heat from one of these is all that is needed to keep the rice nicely warmed through. Finally, the only disturbance the rice should ever need is right at the end, when it can be fluffed through with a fork just before serving.

This is the most basic way of cooking rice. Any number of herbs, spices and flavourings can be added but, most important of all, do not neglect simple salt and freshly ground black pepper.

Home-Made Wholewheat Pasta

450 g (1 lb) wholewheat flour
2 teaspoons salt
3 standard (No. 4) eggs
1 egg yolk
1 tablespoon oil
About 4 tablespoons water

Put the flour and salt into a heap on a working surface. Make a good-sized well in the centre and break in the eggs and yolk. Spoon in the oil and 3 tablespoons of water. Using a quick, stirring motion with the fingers of one hand, gradually erode the walls of the well and incorporate them into the egg mixture. Continue until you have a fairly stiff paste and then work in larger amounts of the surrounding flour until the dough is stiff enough to knead. If it seems very dry and there is still a fair amount of flour to work in, sprinkle the additional water over the dough and knead until all the flour is incorporated into a *firm* dough. Knead this for 10 minutes, by which time it should be silky smooth. Invert a bowl over the dough and leave for about 30 minutes.

Divide the dough in half and roll it out on a lightly-floured work surface until it is uniformly paper-thin all over. Keep a wary eye on it, checking that no portion of the dough is sticking to the surface, then cover it with a clean cloth and leave for a further 30 minutes.

For the simplest pasta, lightly flour your hands and pass them over the surface of the rolled-out dough. Roll it up, swiss-roll style, brushing off any surplus flour adhering to the underside. Now slice the dough across, in ½ cm (¼ in) strips for fettucine or 1 cm (½ in) for tagliatelle. Unroll the slices immediately and leave to dry in separate strips on clean kitchen towels. Repeat the process with the remaining dough if required, if not it can be refrigerated happily for 3 days if it is closely wrapped in cling film or it will deep freeze. For lasagne, cut the dough into rectangles of about 5 × 13 cm (2 × 5 in;) for cannelloni, you will need rectangles of about 7·5 × 10 cm

(3 × 4 in). Leave the dough shapes to dry separately on kitchen towels or paper until you are ready to cook them.

Bring to the boil a large pan of salted water to which you have also added a tablespoon of oil. It will need about 5–10 seconds after the water has returned to the boil to cook all types of fresh pasta strips. To serve the tagliatelle or fettucine, drain in a colander and meanwhile quickly heat some olive oil— about 4 tablespoons to 225 g ($\frac{1}{2}$ lb) of pasta—in the dry pan, together with crushed garlic and seasonings. Toss the pasta in this and serve with melted butter and Parmesan cheese or the sauce of your choice.

For the fresh lasagne or cannelloni, drain the cooked strips in a colander, sluice with cold water and lay in separate layers on kitchen paper to drain. They are now ready to be used.

If you wish to store your pasta, let it dry out on the kitchen towels. Store uncovered, in a cool dry place and use within a month, exactly as you would the bought variety. When you cook it, allow several minutes in boiling salted water.

Fresh Tomato Sauce   (*Serves 2–4*)

350 g (12 oz) fresh tomatoes
110 g (4 oz) green olives
1 tablespoon drained capers
4 tablespoons olive oil
1 fat clove garlic
½ teaspoon rock salt
1 teaspoon black peppercorns
1 fresh chilli
2 heaped tablespoons parsley, chopped

Skin the tomatoes, either by immersing them in boiling water
for a minute or by spearing each one with a fork and holding it
over a gas flame until the skin bursts. Chop the flesh and
transfer, with any juices, to a bowl.

Pit and chop the olives; minimally chop the capers. Add,
with the olive oil, to the tomatoes.

Combine the peeled garlic, salt and peppercorns in a mortar.
Trim the stalk from the chilli and slit in half lengthways.
Sluice out the seeds under cold running water. Chop in pieces
before adding to the mortar and pounding everything to a paste.
Stir into the tomato mixture with the chopped parsley, then
taste again and adjust the seasoning if necessary.

Cook the pasta in plenty of boiling, salted water until *al
dente*. Drain quickly and thoroughly, then return the spaghetti
to the hot pan and toss with the tomato mixture. Serve immediately on piping-hot plates with copious quantities of
Parmesan cheese to sprinkle over the pasta.

Pungent Walnut Sauce (*Serves 2–4*)

50 g (1¾ oz) tin anchovies
4 tablespoons olive oil
450 g (1 lb) tomatoes
50 g (2 oz) walnut pieces
110 g (4 oz) button mushrooms
4 rounded tablespoons parsley, chopped
1 clove garlic, crushed
Salt and freshly ground black pepper

Cook the spaghetti in plenty of boiling, salted water until *al dente;* meanwhile prepare the sauce.

Put the anchovies and their oil in a small saucepan. Add the additional olive oil and heat gently until the anchovies disintegrate.

Peel the tomatoes and chop the flesh. Chop the walnuts fairly finely. Trim and wipe the mushrooms with a piece of damp kitchen paper, then finely chop. Add the tomatoes, walnuts, mushrooms, chopped parsley and crushed garlic to the pan containing the anchovies and oil. Heat just long enough to bring the sauce up to a serveable temperature—it is not necessary to *cook* the ingredients. Taste and season with salt and freshly ground black pepper if necessary.

Drain the spaghetti thoroughly and transfer to a warmed serving dish. Pour the sauce over the top, toss and serve immediately with plenty of grated Parmesan cheese.

Mushroom, Olive and Pepper Sauce

(*Serves 2–4*)

6 slices streaky bacon
1 onion
1 green pepper
6–8 black olives
225 g (8 oz) button mushrooms
56 g (2 oz) tin anchovies in oil
3 tablespoons parsley, chopped
2–3 tablespoons olive oil
Salt and freshly ground black pepper

Remove the rind and cut the bacon slices across into strips. Peel and dice the onion, halve, de-seed and dice the pepper. Pit the olives and roughly chop them. The mushrooms need only to have their stalks trimmed and be wiped with damp kitchen paper before cutting them in wedges, like a cake.

Heat a frying pan without adding oil or fat and, when it is hot, fry the bacon bits until shrivelled and crispy. Using a draining spoon, remove them to a piece of kitchen paper and leave aside.

Fry the diced onion and pepper in the remaining fat until they are softened but not browned. Stir in the mushrooms, drain the oil from the tin of anchovies into the pan, chop the anchovies and add with the parsley. Cover the pan (with a plate if it has no lid) and cook gently for 10 minutes.

Meanwhile, cook the spaghetti in boiling, salted water until *al dente*. When ready, drain in a colander. Immediately warm the olive oil with a little salt and freshly ground black pepper in the hot pan, return the pasta to it and toss using two forks. Quickly stir the chopped olives and reserved bacon pieces into the sauce and cook just long enough to heat through. This can be cooking while you marshal the plates and dole out the spaghetti. Spoon the sauce over the pasta and serve *pronto* with grated Parmesan cheese.

Mackerel, Tomato and Fresh Pepper Sauce

It is best to serve this sauce with *conchiglie* (little shells), whose shape neatly collects and delivers the pieces of fish and sauce to the mouth. (Very clever these Italians!) But, if there is no delicatessen or specialist food shop to sell this type of pasta to you, good old spaghetti will do as second best.

1 small mackerel, filleted
1 small red pepper
1 small green pepper
1 medium onion
56 g (2 oz) tin anchovies in oil
2–3 tablespoons olive oil
397 g (14 oz) tin tomatoes
1 clove garlic, crushed
Salt and freshly ground black pepper
2 teaspoons tomato paste

Wipe the fish and cut into 2·5 cm (1 in) pieces. Seed and chop both the peppers; peel and chop the onion.

Drain the oil from the tin of anchovies into a saucepan and add a further tablespoon of olive oil. Gently fry the chopped vegetables until softened but not coloured. Add the tomatoes, the crushed garlic and a little salt and freshly ground black pepper. Cover and simmer gently for 15 minutes. Uncover and cook for a further 5 minutes before stirring in the tomato paste, followed by the mackerel and chopped anchovy fillets.

Meanwhile, boil the pasta. The instant it reaches the *al dente* stage, drain and toss quickly in a little warmed olive oil and seasoning. Toss the sauce and pasta together and serve quickly on warmed plates. Eat with plenty of Parmesan cheese sprinkled over the lot.

Noodles Baked with Mushrooms and Cream Cheese (*Serves 4*)

1 Spanish onion
225 g (8 oz) button mushrooms
225 g (8 oz) green ribbon noodles
3 tablespoons olive oil
3 tablespoons parsley, chopped
Salt and freshly ground black pepper
80 g (3½ oz) cream cheese flavoured with garlic and *fines herbes*
2 tablespoons dry white breadcrumbs
2 tablespoons Parmesan cheese, grated
25 g (1 oz) butter
Home-made tomato sauce, to serve

Pre-heat the oven to 190 °C (375 °F/mark 5)

Peel and chop the onion; trim the mushroom stalks and wipe with damp kitchen paper then slice thinly.

Cook the noodles in boiling, salted water until they are just a little softer than the *al dente* stage.

Meanwhile, heat the oil in a separate, fairly large saucepan and fry the onion until softened and golden. Stir in the mushrooms and cook over a fairly high heat for 3 or 4 minutes. Turn off the heat under the pan and sprinkle in the parsley and some salt and freshly ground black pepper.

Quickly drain the cooked noodles and transfer to the pan containing the mushroom mixture. Add the cream cheese, clap on the lid and leave aside for about 3 minutes to give the cheese time to melt. Toss the contents of the pan with two forks, taste and season, if necessary.

Transfer the noodles to a deep, buttered baking dish and sprinkle with the combined Parmesan and breadcrumbs. Dot the surface with butter and bake in the top half of the oven for 10–15 minutes or until tinged with brown on top. Serve hot with a home-made tomato sauce.

Cannelloni with Spinach and Curd Cheese Stuffing   (*Serves 5–6*)

Filling:
700 g (1½ lb) fresh, or 2 × 225 g (8 oz) packets frozen, whole-leaf spinach
1 onion
1 tablespoon oil
10 g (½ oz) butter
25 g (1 oz) pine nuts or chopped almonds
175 g (6 oz) curd cheese
75 g (3 oz) grated Parmesan cheese
2 cloves garlic, crushed
2 standard (No. 4) eggs, beaten
Freshly grated nutmeg
Salt and freshly ground black pepper

Pasta:
½ the quantity of home-made wholewheat pasta as shown on page 96, from which you should obtain sixteen 7·5 × 10 cm (3 × 4 in) squares

Sauce:
40 g (1½ oz) wholewheat flour
40 g (1½ oz) butter
425 ml (¾ pint) milk
3 tablespoons yoghurt

Topping:
25 g (1 oz) Parmesan cheese
25 g (1 oz) butter

If you are using fresh spinach, discard any wilted or discoloured leaves and all the stems. Wash in a bowl in several changes of cold water, until no trace of soil is left clinging to the leaves. Transfer the wet leaves directly into a large saucepan and sprinkle with ½ teaspoon of salt. Cover and cook with no additional water for about 5 minutes, stirring once or twice, or until all the leaves are wilted. Drain in a colander and, when sufficiently cool, squeeze the leaves to remove most of the moisture, chop roughly and transfer to a bowl. If using the frozen variety, let it thaw first, squeeze dry and chop.

Peel and finely chop the onion. In a medium pan heat the oil and butter. Stir in the onion and cook until softened and golden. Sprinkle in the pine nuts or almonds and continue cooking until they, too, become lightly coloured. Add to the bowl containing the spinach. Beat in the curd and Parmesan cheeses, the crushed garlic and beaten eggs. Flavour with freshly grated nutmeg and season with salt and freshly ground black pepper.

Prepare and cook the wholewheat pasta as described in the basic recipe (see page 96) and have the pasta rectangles ready, draining on kitchen paper.

Pre-heat the oven to 200 °C (400 °F/mark 6).

Lay the pasta out flat on a work surface and spread each piece with some of the spinach stuffing. Roll up each strip from its longer side, not too tightly. Have ready a liberally buttered ovenproof dish measuring approximately 32 × 20 × 5 cm (13 × 8 × 2 in). You can pack the filled cannelloni fairly tightly into the dish, but keep them in a single layer.

To make the sauce, combine the flour, butter and milk together in a medium saucepan and bring to the boil, stirring briskly. Boil gently for 2 or 3 minutes then remove the pan from the heat. Stir in the yoghurt, taste and flavour with freshly grated nutmeg, salt and freshly ground black pepper. Carefully spoon the sauce over the cannelloni so that no portion of pasta remains uncovered by the sauce. Sprinkle with the remaining 25 g (1 oz) of Parmesan and dot with butter. Bake in the top half of the oven for 20 minutes or until the top has formed a light golden crust. Serve hot with a green salad and additional yoghurt and grated cheese for everyone to help themselves.

Note: If you want to adapt this recipe and use bought cannelloni, I suggest you cook it whole and then slit the tubes open. Lay the filling in the centre and re-form to a tube shape. You will go mad if you try to get the filling into those tubes any other way!

Macaroni Cheese with Bacon and Onion

(Serves 5–6)

This dish has suffered at the hands of cooks in the past because what was served in the name of Macaroni Cheese was usually tasteless and rather stodgy due to an over-abundance of pasta. To be successful, the sauce must be really gutsy, and well-flavoured with a strong Cheddar cheese—as strong as you can buy.

2 medium onions
4 slices streaky bacon
25 g (1 oz) butter
40 g (1½ oz) wholewheat flour
1 teaspoon dry mustard powder
425 ml (¾ pint) milk
1 clove garlic, crushed
110 g (4 oz) strong Cheddar cheese, grated
3 tablespoons yoghurt
Salt and freshly ground black pepper
350 g (12 oz) wholewheat short-cut macaroni

Topping:
25 g (1 oz) Cheddar cheese, grated
25 g (1 oz) fresh wholemeal breadcrumbs
10 g (½ oz) butter

Pre-heat the oven to 200 °C (400 °F/mark 6)

Peel and chop the onions. Rind and cut the bacon across into striplets.

In a medium saucepan heat the butter until frothy. Stir in the chopped onion and bacon strips and cook gently for about 10 minutes or until the onion is softened and lightly golden. Sprinkle in the flour and mustard. Stir and continue to cook over a low heat for a minute before gradually adding the milk. Bring to the boil stirring, before flavouring with the crushed clove of garlic. Then leave to simmer very gently, uncovered, for 10 minutes. Remove the pan from the heat and stir in the grated cheese and yoghurt. Taste and season well with salt and freshly ground black pepper. Remember that the pasta will act as a tremendous blanket on the flavour so it needs to have a good strong taste. Cover and keep hot.

Boil the macaroni in salted water, according to the instructions on the packet. Drain it thoroughly in a colander, jumping it up and down to get the water out. Transfer to a bowl and mix thoroughly with the sauce. Taste and season again if necessary.

Transfer the mixture to a buttered baking dish and sprinkle the mixed cheese and breadcrumbs over the top. Finally, dot the surface with small flecks of butter. Bake in the top half of the oven for 25–30 minutes. Serve hot.

Brown Saffron Rice   (*Serves 4*)

This is really just a basic recipe to play around with to your heart's content. Add browned nuts, raisins, currants, herbs, cheese, etc., as your fancy takes you. Your local chemist is about the most reliable place to buy quality saffron strands.

1 medium onion
2 tablespoons oil
1 mug brown rice
2 mugs stock and dry cider mixed
¼ teaspoon saffron strands
About 1 tablespoon lemon juice
Salt and freshly ground black pepper
25 g (1 oz) butter

Peel and chop the onion, then fry gently in the oil in a medium saucepan until softened but not browned. Stir in the rice and cook for 2 minutes before pouring in the stock and cider. Sprinkle with the saffron, bring to simmering point, then cover and cook gently for 40–45 minutes or until the rice is just tender and all the liquid is absorbed. Fork in the lemon juice and salt and freshly ground black pepper to taste. Dot with butter, cover the pan with a folded tea towel and lid and leave aside in a warm place for 5 minutes before serving.

Brown Rice with Grapes (*Serves 4*)

This goes particularly well with light meats: chicken, pork or veal.

1 onion
225 g (8 oz) black grapes
10 g (½ oz) butter
1 tablespoon oil
50 g (2 oz) pine nuts
1 mug brown rice
2 scant mugs boiling chicken stock
Bouquet garni (2 sprigs thyme, 1 bayleaf, 3 sprigs parsley)
Salt and freshly ground black pepper

Pre-heat the oven to 180 °C (350 °F/mark 4)

Peel and dice the onion; peel, halve and de-seed the grapes.

Heat the butter and oil in a fireproof casserole. Fry the onion in the hot fat until softened and golden. Stir in the pine nuts and cook, stirring constantly until they are evenly and lightly browned.

Pour the measured rice into a sieve and sluice thoroughly with cold water. Drain, and transfer the rice to the casserole, stirring it in well to coat all the grains with butter and oil. Continue to heat for a couple of minutes before adding the stock. Bring to simmering point, add the bouquet garni, cover and transfer to the oven to bake for about 45 minutes or until the rice is tender (but still a little chewy) and has absorbed all the stock. Discard the bouquet garni and fork in the grapes. Taste and season with salt and freshly ground black pepper. Re-cover and leave aside for 5 minutes to allow the grapes time to heat through. Serve hot.

Green Herbed Rice   (*Serves 4–5*)

Instead of butter, the hot rice can be served with curd cheese or a soft, white cheese (e.g. Wensleydale) crumbled over the surface. If using a cheese topping, add it before covering the pan and leaving the rice aside for 10 minutes: this will give it plenty of time to melt. Left-overs are nice served cold, mixed with a little vinaigrette or served with a garlicky mayonnaise.

8 spring onions with plenty of green tops
50 g (2 oz) prepared spinach leaves
Scant 700 ml (1¼ pints) stock or water
350 ml (12 fl oz) brown rice
2 heaped tablespoons chopped fresh herbs (thyme, rosemary,
    sage, savory, marjoram, tarragon, etc.)
Grated rind of ½ lemon
1 teaspoon rock salt
½ teaspoon black peppercorns
1 clove garlic
Generous squeeze of lemon juice
25 g (1 oz) butter

Trim the spring onions top and bottom and finely chop with the spinach leaves.

Bring a saucepan containing the stock or water to the boil and trickle the rice into it in a slow, steady stream. Adjust the heat to give a bare simmer, then cover and cook gently for about 40 minutes or until all the liquid has been absorbed and the rice is just tender.

Fork the chopped onions, spinach leaves, herbs and lemon rind into the rice. Crush the salt, peppercorns and garlic together and fork in also. Cover the pan with a thickly-folded tea towel and leave aside in a warm place for 10 minutes. Just before serving sprinkle with the lemon juice and dot with flicks of butter.

Brown Rice with Mushrooms and Tomatoes   (*Serves 4–6*)

This is a vegetable dish to accompany a main course but it can be served as a dish in its own right if transferred to a baking dish, sprinkled with a mixture of grated cheese and brown breadcrumbs and either baked or quickly grilled.

1 large onion
225 g (8 oz) button mushrooms
397 g (14 oz) tin tomatoes or 450 g (1 lb) fresh tomatoes
4 tablespoons oil
425 ml (15 fl oz) brown rice
700 ml (1¼ pints) boiling stock or water
1 clove garlic, crushed
1 dessertspoon fresh chopped thyme
Salt and freshly ground black pepper

Peel and chop the onion; wipe the mushrooms with a piece of damp kitchen paper, trim the stalks and slice thinly. If using fresh tomatoes, peel them first and then chop coarsely.

Heat *half* the oil in a medium pan and stir in *half* the quantity of chopped onion and all the sliced mushrooms. Cook for 3 or 4 minutes before stirring in the rice. Let the rice colour up a little before pouring in the boiling stock or water. Bring to simmering point, then cover and cook over a low heat for 40 minutes or until the rice is just tender and the liquid is absorbed.

Meanwhile, heat the remaining oil in a separate, smaller pan and fry the remaining onion until softened but not browned. Add the crushed garlic and the tomatoes and leave to simmer gently, uncovered, for about 30 minutes or until reduced to a thickish sauce.

Fork the hot tomato sauce and chopped thyme into the rice. Taste and season with salt and freshly ground black pepper. Then cover the pan with a folded, clean tea towel and leave aside in a warm place for about 10 minutes. Serve hot.

Indian Style Spiced Rice   (*Serves 2 or 4*)

A good dish to serve with nicely spiced lentil or meat rissoles. You can also make it a main-meal dish simply by forking in quartered hard-boiled eggs or lightly fried liver strips, which should be added just before serving.

1 large onion
50 g (2 oz) butter
1 mug long-grain brown rice
2 teaspoons ground turmeric
2·5 cm (1 in) cinnamon stick
4 cloves
1 teaspoon cummin seeds
2–2½ mugs hot stock, vegetable or chicken
Salt and freshly ground black pepper
50 g (2 oz) almonds, blanched and toasted

Garnish:
Chopped parsley
Natural yoghurt

Peel and chop the onion. In a medium saucepan melt the butter until frothy, then stir in the chopped onion and cook over a moderate heat for 3 or 4 minutes until lightly browned. Add the rice and stir until the grains glisten with butter. Cook for a further minute or two to toast the grains a little. Add the spices, stir, and pour in the stock. Bring to simmering point, cover and cook gently for about 45 minutes. By this time the rice should be pleasantly chewy and have absorbed all the liquid. If you prefer the rice a little more cooked, add a further 3 or 4 tablespoons of hot water and continue cooking. Taste and season with salt and freshly ground black pepper. Pull the saucepan off the heat, put a clean, folded teacloth over the pan and the lid on top and leave aside for 5 minutes before serving. Fork the almonds into rice and serve sprinkled with chopped parsley and yoghurt dolloped on top.

Vegetable Risotto (*Serves 6*)

The vegetables can, of course, be swopped around according to what is available.

225 g (8 oz) green beans, haricot or runner
110 g (4 oz) cabbage
3 courgettes
2 carrots
2 potatoes
1 large onion
4 slices bacon, streaky
60 g (2½ oz) butter
2 tablespoons oil
2 mugs brown rice
2 mugs stock
2 mugs tomato juice
2 large cloves garlic, crushed
Salt and freshly ground black pepper

Garnish:
2 heaped tablespoons parsley, chopped
Parmesan cheese, grated
25 g (1 oz) butter

Pre-heat the oven to 180 °C (350 °F/mark 4)

First prepare the vegetables. String and cut the beans into 2·5 cm (1 in) lengths. Rinse and finely slice the cabbage leaves. Halve the courgettes lengthways, then across into slices about ¾ cm (⅓ in) thick. Similarly, scrub, then quarter, the carrots lengthways before slicing ½ cm (¼ in) thick across. Scrub and cut potatoes into roughly 1 cm (½ in) cubes. Peel and dice the onion, rind and dice the bacon.

Combine the butter and oil in a large flameproof casserole. When the butter has melted, stir in the bacon pieces and cook until the fat runs from the sizzling bacon. Add the prepared vegetables to the pan. Stir and cook until they have lost their initial crispness, then add the rice. Stir and cook for 2 minutes more, then pour in the stock and tomato juice, add the crushed garlic, and some salt and freshly ground black pepper. Bring to simmering point, then transfer to the oven to cook uncovered for 35 minutes. Remove from the oven, sprinkle thickly with parsley and Parmesan cheese and dot with butter. Cover and leave aside for 5–10 minutes in a warm place before serving.

BEANS, PEAS
AND LENTILS

This chapter has been a revelation to me. I always used to think that dried peas, beans and lentils needed lengthy soaking before cooking; my menus were never planned far enough ahead to cope with this, so I never really got to grips with the problem. Then my interest in wholefoods developed and so began the enquiry into the rigmarole surrounding the cooking of pulses. The first thing I immediately discovered was the wide disparity in methods adopted by the various cookery books. It seemed to me that the older the cookery book, the longer were the soaking and cooking times given. Furthermore, when driven to testing these things out for myself, I found that my results did not tally with anyone else's!

First let me say that 'slow but sure' wins the day. In other words, if you soak beans for 8–12 hours in cold water they will double in size and weight. If you are an organised cook, always allow for this and soak pulses in *plenty* of cold water.

However, if, like me, you often need to save time, then the following relative short cuts are open to you. The beans won't gain so much in size and weight, but you'll be able to use them much sooner.

(a) Pour boiling water on to the dried pulses and then soak for 2 hours.

(b) Put the pulses into cold water with any flavouring or herbs you fancy, bring to the boil, boil for 2–3 minutes, then pull the pan off the heat, cover and leave aside for 1 hour.

(c) Put the unsoaked pulses into a pressure cooker with cold water (usually a ratio of 450 g/1 lb of pulses to 570 ml/1 pint of water), bring up to pressure and steam for 35 minutes at 15 lb pressure. (This applies to the conventional type of pressure cooker: there are some new, rather different models on the market, so do consult the instruction booklet first.)

Remember that, whatever method you use—with the exception of pressure cooking—the cooking times will vary: the rule is simply that the longer you soak your pulses the less cooking they need.

Any of the soaking methods described will suit any kind of

dried bean (white, black, brown, red, rose, coco, chick peas, black-eyed peas, etc.), *except* lentils and split peas: these need neither soaking nor pressure cooking, which is inadvisable.

Some cookery books advise you to throw out the soaking liquid and bring the pulses to the boil in fresh water. They occasionally comment that this will minimise flatulence, but according to medical opinion the effect would be negligible, so I leave it to you.

Should you salt the boiling water? It does seem to slow down the softening process a little, so I suggest that you add it at the very end.

As for the time each type of legume will take to cook, it is very hard to say. In my recipes, I have usually plumped for cooking method (*b*), but you may find that the batch you cook takes some time more or less than I have stated, depending on where the pulses come from and how long ago they were dried.

The great thing is that pulses are reaching us ever faster from their countries of origin, and this can only increase their popularity. They are a marvellous standby in the kitchen—an excellent store-cupboard item that can be turned into incredibly diverse and satisfying meals. The more we latch on to the idea of using them, the nearer we shall come to learning their full potential.

Butter Beans in Lemon and Parsley Sauce

(*Serves 4–6*)

225 g (8 oz) butter beans, soaked overnight
Bouquet garni

Sauce:
25 g (1 oz) fresh parsley
25 g (1 oz) butter
25 g (1 oz) wholewheat flour
275 ml ($\frac{1}{2}$ pint) milk
Grated rind of $\frac{1}{2}$ lemon
2 teaspoons lemon juice
Salt and freshly ground black pepper

Garnish:
1 tablespoon wheatgerm
3–4 teaspoons yoghurt

Drain the soaked beans and put in a large saucepan with the bouquet garni and plenty of fresh cold water to cover. Bring to the boil, cover and simmer gently until the beans are tender but not disintegrating (this usually takes $1\frac{1}{2}$–2 hours). Drain the cooked beans, discarding the bouquet garni, and put on one side while preparing the sauce.

Put the parsley in a sieve and sluice well with cold water. Drain, then dry the sprigs thoroughly on kitchen paper before chopping finely.

Using the same pan, heat and mix the butter, flour and milk, stirring constantly and quickly with a spoon. Once the sauce boils, turn down the heat and add the parsley and lemon rind and juice. Return the drained beans to re-heat in the sauce, taste and season with salt and freshly ground black pepper.

Pour into a serving dish and sprinkle with the wheatgerm. Blob the yoghurt over the top and stir briefly to give a marbled effect. Serve hot.

Honied Black-Eyed Susies (*Serves 6–8*)

Americans call these beans Black-Eyed Susies or Black-Eyed Peas because of the distinctive black spot on each. Here, they make a substantial dish to serve with sausages, pork, boiled or baked gammon or bacon.

450 g (1 lb) black-eyed peas
450 g (1 lb) slab of salted streaky bacon, or thickly sliced
  streaky bacon
1 large onion
110 g (4 oz) crystallised ginger
10 g (½ oz) butter
1 tablespoon oil
2 tablespoons home-made chutney
2 teaspoons dry mustard
Freshly ground black pepper
2 tablespoons clear honey

Put the peas in a large saucepan with plenty of cold water to cover. Bring to the boil, boil for 2 minutes then remove from the heat. Cover and leave aside for about 1 hour. Then bring back to the boil and cook gently for 45 minutes.

Meanwhile, rind the bacon and cut into 1 cm (½ in) cubes. Peel and dice the onion and chop the crystallised ginger.

Heat the butter and oil in a large casserole and fry the bacon cubes until the fat begins to run from them. Stir in the onion and continue to cook until it is softened and golden. Stir in the chopped ginger.

Heat the oven to 170 °C (325 °F/mark 3).

When the beans are just tender, drain and stir them into the casserole with the chutney blended with the mustard powder. Season with some freshly ground black pepper; it is unlikely that the dish will need any salt as there should be enough from the bacon. Drizzle the honey over the beans, then cover and bake for 1 hour. Give the beans a stir and taste, seasoning if necessary. Return the casserole to the oven to bake for a further 30 minutes or until the beans are dry. Serve hot.

Black Beans with Rum   (*Serves 6*)

Delicious served with smoked ham, boiled bacon or pickled or spiced meats.

450 (1 lb) black beans
Bouquet garni (bayleaf, thyme, parsley)
1 large onion
3 stalks celery
2 carrots
40 g (1½ oz) butter
6 tablespoons dark rum
1 heaped tablespoon dark brown sugar
2 large cloves garlic, crushed
1 tablespoon molasses or black treacle
Salt and freshly ground black pepper
Chilled yoghurt or soured cream, to serve

Rinse the beans with cold water in a sieve or colander then transfer them to a large saucepan with plenty of cold water to cover. Bring to the boil, boil for 1 or 2 minutes then cover and leave aside for 1 hour. Add the bouquet garni, bring back to the boil, cover and simmer gently for 30 minutes.

Meanwhile, prepare the vegetables. Peel and chop the onion, scrub and dice the celery and carrots.

When the beans are just tender drain in a colander, reserving the cooking liquor but discarding the bouquet garni. Return the hot dry pan to the heat and melt the butter. Gently fry the vegetables in the foaming butter until softened and lightly coloured. Return the beans to the pan with 275 ml (½ pint) of their liquor, and add the rum, sugar, crushed garlic and molasses. Bring back to simmering point and cook covered for a further 35 minutes or until both beans and vegetables are tender. Taste and season well with salt and freshly ground black pepper. Serve each piping hot portion of beans with a dollop of yoghurt or soured cream on top.

Mexican Refried Beans (*Serves 4*)

A useful way of using up any left-over beans, but if you want to make this in a hurry put the unsoaked, rinsed beans in a pressure cooker with 570 ml (1 pint) of water and steam at 15 lb pressure for 30–40 minutes.

1 onion
Large clove garlic
1 teaspoon sea salt
About 6 tablespoons olive oil
½–1 teaspoon chilli powder
225 g (8 oz) cooked kidney beans (reserve the cooking liquor if possible)

Peel and chop the onion, peel the clove of garlic and crush with the sea salt. Heat 2 tablespoons of the oil in a frying pan and stir in the chopped onion. Allow it to colour and soften before adding the crushed garlic, salt and ½ teaspoon of chilli powder.

Mash the kidney beans down slightly, adding a tablespoon or two of cooking liquor or water if the mixture is rather stiff. Stir in the contents of the frying pan. Taste and season, adding more chilli at this stage if you like. Add a further 2 tablespoons of oil to the frying pan and heat. Turn the bean mixture into the hot oil and pat out to a flat cake. Once the mixture has had a chance to brown slightly on the underside, start shovelling it over and over in the pan, adding more oil as and when necessary, until it is good and hot.

Serve as a side dish, sprinkled with grated cheese or some thinly sliced raw onion if liked.

Hashed Bean Cakes (*Serves 4*)

This recipe uses the previous one as its base up until the stage before frying the mixture in oil.

1 recipe Mexican Refried Beans (see page 121)
Plus:
1 onion
25 g (1 oz) grated cheese
6 2·5 cm (1 in) cubes Mozzarella cheese
About 75 g (3 oz) dry brown breadcrumbs
Oil for shallow frying

Peel and chop the onion very finely and add this additional amount of uncooked onion to the Mexican Refined Bean mixture. Sprinkle in the cheese; mix and taste for seasoning. Chill the mixture in the refrigerator.

Divide the bean mixture into six, then shape the portions into patties, burying a cube of the Mozzarella cheese in the centre of each. Coat the cakes in the dry breadcrumbs, pushing them gently but firmly on to each pattie. Fry the bean cakes slowly in about ½ cm (¼ in) of oil until piping hot throughout, so the Mozzarella in the centre has a chance to melt.

Serve with a spicy home-made tomato sauce on a mound of buttered noodles or with very creamy mashed potatoes.

Lentils in Cider (*Serves 4*)

A dry cider is best and real 'scrumpy' would be nice, but you could use any home-made, red or white wine. If you do use wine it is the one occasion I would bother to soak the lentils in boiling water for about 2 hours, then drain and use as in the recipe, but use *half* the quantity of wine because a whole pint, even if home-made, does seem rather excessive. Serve the lentils with pork, spicy sausages, omelettes, etc.

1 large onion
1 large carrot
2 slices streaky bacon
Bouquet garni (whole clove of garlic, 2 sprigs parsley,
    2 sprigs thyme, 1 bayleaf)
1 tablespoon oil
225 g (8 oz) brown lentils
570 ml (1 pint) dry cider
Salt and freshly ground black pepper

Peel and cut the onion in half, then into about 6 wedges, and separate all the layers. Top, tail and scrub the carrot then cut across in slices about 3 mm ($\frac{1}{8}$ in) thick. Rind and cut the bacon in half lengthways, then across to form striplets. Make up the bouquet garni and bash once or twice with a rolling pin to bruise the herbs.

Heat the oil in a medium saucepan and stir in the bacon strips. Cook until the fat runs before stirring in the onion and carrot. Brown the vegetables slightly, then add the lentils. Stir and cook for a minute or two, then pour in the cider and tuck the bouquet garni well down in amongst the lentils. Bring to simmering point, then cover and cook very gently for about 1 hour. If you are using wine and have therefore soaked the lentils beforehand, they might need only 35 minutes to cook. When soft, but still holding their shape, the lentils should have absorbed almost all the liquid. If not, turn up the heat and boil rapidly, shaking the pan until the liquid has practically all evaporated. Taste and season with salt and freshly ground black pepper.

Note: If serving with pork, snip in some dried apple rings during cooking.

Yellow Split Peas with Coriander (*Serves 4*)

Try serving these mashed peas as hot as possible, piled in a small mound in the centre of each plate. Spoon a generous amount of yoghurt over each portion and serve, in summer surrounded by a crisp lettuce salad and olives, or in winter with a spinach and bacon salad.

½ teaspoon sea salt
1 teaspoon mustard seeds
1 teaspoon coriander seeds
1 fat clove garlic
225 g (½ lb) yellow split peas
425 ml (¾ pint) water or vegetable stock
1 onion
3–6 tablespoons olive oil
3 tablespoons chopped coriander leaves, or parsley

Put the sea salt, mustard and coriander seeds and the garlic clove together in a mortar and pound to a pulpy mass. Transfer the mixture to a saucepan and add the peas and stock or water. Bring to simmering point then cover and cook gently until the peas are absolutely tender and the liquid for the most part absorbed; this should not take more than about 45 minutes. If the peas are still a little undercooked at this stage and the liquid all but gone, simply add a few tablespoons of water and carry on cooking.

Meanwhile, peel and halve the onion and slice it across thinly. Heat 3 tablespoons of oil in a separate saucepan and fry the onion gently, stirring frequently until well browned and crispy.

When the peas are tender, mash the contents of the pan to a pulp using a potato masher. Stir in the fried onion and any oil remaining in the pan, plus the chopped coriander, or parsley. Add sufficient additional olive oil to give the mixture the consistency of soft mashed potatoes. Taste and season if necessary, and serve hot.

Red Kidney Beans in Tomato Wine Sauce   (*Serves 4*)

Eat this as a vegetarian dish with brown rice or as it stands with grilled or roast meats. It is also good with some smoked sausage sliced up and cooked in it! Whatever way you choose, top it off with yoghurt.

225 g (8 oz) dried red kidney beans, soaked overnight

Sauce:
1 Spanish onion
1 large green pepper
3 tablespoons oil
396 g (14 oz) tin tomatoes
1 teaspoon dried basil
1 clove garlic, crushed
150 ml (¼ pint) red wine
2 teaspoons tomato paste
Salt and freshly ground black pepper

Drain the beans and cover with plenty of fresh cold water. Bring to the boil, cover and cook for 30 minutes. Drain.

Meanwhile, peel and chop the onion; halve, de-seed and dice the green pepper.

Heat the oil in the same rinsed-out pan. Fry the onion until softened and golden. Add the tomatoes, basil, crushed garlic, diced pepper and wine. Stir in the beans, bring to simmering point and continue to cook until the beans are absolutely tender and bathed in a nice sauce. Stir in the tomato paste and taste and season with salt and freshly ground black pepper. Serve hot.

Barley and Mushroom Pilaff   (*Serves 4–6*)

A dish that will happily accompany most of the light meats or can be served on its own on a bed of spinach. Try baking pork chops on top of the pilaff: start by browning them first in the oil, then put aside until the cream is stirred in. Lay the chops on top and continue baking as in the recipe. Very good!

1 very large onion
450 g (1 lb) cap mushrooms
3 tablespoons oil
225 g (8 oz) pearl barley
¾ teaspoon dried dill weed
Salt and freshly ground black pepper
570 ml (1 pint) vegetable or chicken stock
150 ml (¼ pint) soured cream
Generous squeeze of lemon juice

Pre-heat the oven to 180 °C (350 °F/mark 4)

Peel and halve the onion. Cut each half in half again and slice across thinly. Prepare the mushrooms by trimming the stems and wiping the caps over with a piece of damp kitchen paper. Cut the mushrooms into wedges according to size, small caps into four, larger ones into six or eight.

Heat the oil in a large flameproof casserole and stir in the sliced onion. Cook over a moderate heat for about 5 minutes, or until softened and golden. Stir in the mushrooms and cook for a further 3 or 4 minutes then add the barley. Stir and cook for a minute or two before sprinkling in the dill weed, plus a little seasoning, then pouring in the stock. Stir again, bring to boiling point then transfer to the oven to bake, uncovered, for 40 minutes. Remove from the oven and stir in the cream. Taste and add lemon juice and additional salt and freshly ground black pepper as required. Bring back to boiling point, cover with a lid and return the casserole to the oven to bake for a further 30 minutes. Serve piping hot.

Dried Green Pea Purée (*Serves 4–6*)

The applications of this simple recipe are endless. My particular favourites are: serving it mounded up on a plate topped with sausages and a white wine or cider gravy; or spread in individual small bowls and served with a peeled, soft-boiled egg on top and accompanied by fingers of buttered toast; or crisply fried patties of the mixture served with bacon and fried egg. It also makes a good stuffing for poultry, crown of lamb, etc . . . !

1 onion
425 ml (¾ pint) stock or water
1 clove
225 g (½ lb) green split peas
50 g (2 oz) butter or cream
Freshly grated nutmeg
Salt and freshly ground black pepper

Peel and cut the onion into six. Put it into a medium saucepan with the stock or water and bring to the boil. Add the clove and slowly trickle in the split peas. Bring back to simmering point, then cover and cook very gently for ¾–1 hour until the peas are absolutely tender and the liquid absorbed.

Remove the pan from the heat, discard the clove, then either rub the contents through a sieve or mouli, or blend in a liquidiser until smooth. Beat in the butter, a little freshly grated nutmeg and salt and pepper to taste. Serve hot.

Note: Adjust the consistency of the purée according to the way in which it is to be served. To thin it, add cream or top of the milk. If it is too thin for your purposes, add mashed potato or heat in a double saucepan for 20 minutes or so.

Dried Haricot Beans in Fresh Tomato Sauce   (*Serves 6–8*)

450 g (1 lb) dried haricot beans

Sauce:
3 carrots
3 stalks celery
1 large onion
2 large cloves garlic
A handful fresh basil leaves
1 kg 350 g (3 lb) tomatoes
40 g (1½ oz) butter
1 tablespoon oil
½ teaspoon dried oregano
1 teaspoon brown sugar
1 tablespoon tomato paste
Salt and freshly ground black pepper
Fresh basil, to serve

Rinse the beans with cold water and transfer to a large saucepan. Cover with 1¾ litres (3 pints) of cold water and bring to the boil. Boil for 3 minutes then remove the pan from the heat and leave aside, covered, for 1 hour. Bring the beans back to the boil and simmer gently, with the pan ⅞ covered by the fitted lid, for 30 minutes. Drain the beans reserving the liquor.

While the beans cook, prepare the vegetables. Scrub and finely dice the carrots and celery, peel and finely chop the onion. Peel and crush the garlic and chop the basil. Peel the tomatoes either by immersing them in boiling water for 1 minute or by skewering them individually with a fork and holding them over a gas flame until the skins burst; coarsely chop.

Heat the butter and oil in a large pan or fireproof casserole and gently fry the carrots, celery and onion for 10 minutes. Stir in the chopped tomatoes, crushed garlic, oregano and sugar, then the drained beans and 275 ml (½ pint) of the reserved liquor. Bring to simmering point and continue to cook gently uncovered, for 1½ hours. Stir in the basil and tomato paste and carry on cooking for a further 30 minutes. If the mixture seems to be getting a bit too thick, add a little more of the reserved liquor. Taste and season well with salt and freshly ground black pepper. Serve hot with a little extra chopped fresh basil sprinkled over the surface.

Flageolets in Green Bean Purée   (*Serves 4*)

The marriage of these dried beans in a fresh green bean purée produces a lovely, delicately flavoured vegetable that is delicious served with roast lamb.

225 g (8 oz) dried flageolet beans, soaked overnight
1 carrot
1 small onion
1 bayleaf

Purée:
450 g (1 lb) fresh green haricot or bobby beans
About 75 ml (3 fl oz) double cream
25 g (1 oz) butter
A little extra cream or butter
Salt and freshly ground black pepper
Freshly grated nutmeg
A good squeeze of lemon juice

Drain the soaked beans and transfer to a saucepan. Cover with plenty of fresh, cold water and add the chunked carrot, peeled onion and bayleaf. Bring to the boil, cover and simmer gently for 1½–2 hours or until the beans are tender. Drain in a colander, discarding the vegetables and bayleaf.

Meanwhile wash the fresh green beans and top and tail them. Boil in the minimum of salted water for about 8 minutes, until just tender. Drain and transfer to the goblet of a liquidiser and add the butter, cream and *half* the cooked, drained flageolet beans. Whizz to form a smoothish purée; you will probably need to keep stopping the machine to scrape down the mixture

inside the goblet. Return the purée to the saucepan with the remaining cooked flageolets. Re-heat and adjust the consistency
of the purée with more cream or butter to give a soft, velvety
mixture, not at all stiff or stodgy. Taste and flavour with salt,
freshly ground black pepper, freshly grated nutmeg and lemon
juice. Serve hot.

Curried Soy Beans   (*Serves 4–6*)

Soy beans have the highest food value of all the pulses and are
far better eaten in their natural state than cunningly contrived
into little square pieces to resemble meat!

225 g (8 oz) soy beans, soaked overnight
1 onion
2·5 cm (1 in) piece of fresh ginger root
2 fresh green chillies
2 tablespoons oil
1 clove garlic, crushed
1 teaspoon ground cummin
2 teaspoons ground coriander
1 teaspoon turmeric
397 g (14 oz) tin tomatoes
1 dessertspoon molasses or black treacle
Salt and freshly ground black pepper

Drain the beans and put in a saucepan with plenty of fresh
water to cover. Bring to the boil and simmer, covered, for about
1 hour or until the beans have lost their crunch.

Meanwhile, peel and chop the onion; scrape and finely chop
the ginger root. Trim the tops from the chillies, slice lengthways and sluice out the seeds under cold, running water, then
slice very finely.

When the beans are ready, drain them in a colander. In the
dry saucepan heat the oil and fry the onion until softened and
golden. Stir in the ginger and chillies and cook for a minute
or two before adding the crushed garlic, ground cummin,
coriander and turmeric. Stir and cook for a couple of minutes

more, then add the drained soy beans, the tomatoes and finally
stir in the spoonful of molasses or black treacle. Cover and
simmer gently for 30 minutes, then uncover and continue
cooking until the liquid surrounding the beans takes on a good
sauce consistency. Serve hot.

Polenta   (*Serves 4–6*)

Polenta (a sort of corn meal porridge) is to some Italians what
potatoes are to us and it is equally as adaptable. For example,
when piping hot it can be served mixed with butter and Parmesan cheese, or can accompany roast meats, game or stews.
Once cooled and hardened, it makes delicious, very crisp,
fritters when sliced and fried in oil (serve with a tomato or
meat sauce), or sliced, grilled and spread with a soft, tangy,
Blue cheese like Gorgonzola.

275 ml (½ pint) coarse polenta
Salt and freshly ground black pepper

Heat 570 ml (1 pint) of water in the top of a double saucepan
over direct heat until boiling. Also have on hand some boiling
water ready in a kettle.

Turn down the heat so the water is just simmering. Add
the polenta to the pan in a slow steady stream, stirring all the
time. Keep the water at a slow simmer. Transfer the pan to sit
over the bottom half of the double saucepan, half-filled with
boiling water. Season and leave for 20 minutes, stirring
frequently. Beat in more boiling water as required: the polenta
should finally be of a just-pourable consistency. When the
polenta is ready it seems to tear away from the side of the pan
as you stir. If you wish to serve it hot, do so immediately,
otherwise pat it into a shallow, wetted tin and leave to cool and
harden. It will turn out as neat as ninepence for you to slice
and use as desired.

MAIN COURSE
AND
SUPPER DISHES

The aim of the non-vegetarian section is to take a fairly cheap form of first-class protein and spin it out with other, even cheaper foodstuffs to produce a nutritionally balanced dish for a minimum of expenditure. If all that sounds a bit high-flown, it really means getting the most for your money. These dishes range from the straightforward family supper to something impressive to serve to friends.

So, too, with the vegetarian half. Although not a vegetarian myself, I do enjoy the *difference* that a vegetarian meal can offer and cannot understand why some people should take wholesome, natural vegetarian ingredients and dress them up in the guise of meat. At college it was customary to spend hours forming a vegetable mixture into something like a cutlet, cooking it and then, the *pièce de résistance*, decorating it with a cutlet frill! Thank goodness this approach to food is now dying out but there are still traces left. Why, for example, form soya protein into meat-shaped pieces? How much better to serve up vegetarian foods for what they are: ingredients, skilfully cooked to retain the best in flavour, appearance and food value.

VEGETARIAN DISHES

Cheese, Potato and Soured Cream Soufflé (*Serves 4–5*)

A delicious soufflé which, because of the potato, has a lovely, crunchy crust. If the boiled potatoes you use have skins on, simply grate them in, skin and all. I know the amount of butter sounds a lot, but the potato gobbles it up!

110 g (4 oz) strong Cheddar cheese
4 spring onions or a few green leaves of leek
110 g (4 oz) butter
1 clove garlic, crushed
25 g (1 oz) plain wholewheat flour
150 ml (¼ pint) soured cream
4 tablespoons natural yoghurt
5 standard (No. 4) eggs
275 g (10 oz) cold boiled potatoes
Salt and freshly ground black pepper
Freshly grated nutmeg

Pre-heat the oven to 200 °C (400 °F/mark 6)

Grate the cheese, then trim the onions at top and bottom, and chop finely. If using leek leaves simply rinse and chop enough leaves to give a rounded tablespoonful.

Heat the butter in a medium pan and stir in the chopped onion or leek and the crushed clove of garlic. Simmer gently for 3 or 4 minutes before stirring in the flour. Turn the heat down very low and gradually stir in the soured cream and yoghurt. Continue to cook very gently for about 5 minutes or until the sauce is just thick enough to hold a gap when the spoon is scraped through it across the base of the pan; remove from the heat. Separate the eggs, placing the whites together in a clean, grease-free bowl and beating the egg yolks into the sauce. Coarsely grate the potatoes directly into the pan, stopping frequently to beat them in as you work. Lastly, beat in all but 2 tablespoons of the grated cheese.

Whisk the egg whites until stiff but not dry and stir a heaped tablespoonful into the mixture to slacken it, before carefully folding in the rest of the egg white. Taste and season well with salt and freshly ground black pepper and nutmeg.

Pour the mixture into a buttered 1-litre (2 pint) baking dish and sprinkle with the reserved cheese. Bake in the centre of the oven for 50 minutes or until well-risen and golden brown. Test by inserting a skewer in the centre. It is ready if it comes out clean, although I must say I think soufflés are nicest when served still slightly creamy in the centre. Serve immediately.

A home-made tomato sauce is nice served with this, or a spoonful of cream trickled over each portion.

Baked, Stuffed Onions with Cream and Hazelnut Topping
(Serves 4)

I usually serve these onions on a bed of spinach tossed with soy sauce and some chopped, hard-boiled egg. The chopped, roasted hazelnuts I buy ready-prepared in packets obtainable from a very well-known, large supermarket chain!

4 of the largest, best, Spanish onions you can find
About 3 tablespoons olive oil
1 pepper, green or red
4 medium tomatoes
1 clove garlic, crushed
Salt and freshly ground black pepper

Topping:
75 g (3 oz) chopped, roasted hazelnuts
25 g (1 oz) wheatgerm
40 g (1½ oz) grated Parmesan cheese
150 ml (¼ pint) single cream

Pre-heat the oven to 180 °C (350 °F/mark 4)

Peel the onions and cook whole in a large pan of boiling, salted water for 8 minutes. Drain and leave until cool enough to handle. Using a sharp knife, cut a thin cap from the top (shoot end) of each onion, then, using first the knife then your fingers, ease the centres out until you are left with about a 1-cm (½ in) thick onion shell. In doing this you will also create a hole in the base of each onion shell: this does not matter at all. Sit the onions in a deep casserole which has been brushed with some oil.

Take half the onion debris and chop it finely, (keep the rest for other dishes requiring onions). De-seed and finely chop the pepper. Skin the tomatoes, either by immersing in boiling water for a minute or so, or skewering them with a fork and holding over a gas flame, then chop coarsely.

Heat the oil in a medium saucepan and fry the onion and pepper until softened and lightly coloured. Add the tomatoes, cover and cook for about 5 minutes. Uncover and continue cooking until most of the liquid generated by the tomatoes has evaporated. Stir in the crushed garlic and salt and freshly ground black pepper to taste. Fill each onion shell with an equal quantity of mixture.

In a bowl combine all the ingredients for the topping. Season and stir to form a stiffish paste. Give each onion a thick thatch of this mixture, cover the casserole with a lid, making sure it does not touch the topping, and bake in the top half of the oven for about 30 minutes, or until the topping has browned and the onions are piping hot. Serve immediately.

Pea and Mushroom Curry (*Serves 4*)

A nice, quick, supper-type curry, not too arduous to prepare. Serve on a bed of onions and brown rice or, if you are watching your weight, on a bed of spinach or cauliflower sprigs.

450 g (1 lb) mushrooms
3 tomatoes
450 g (1 lb) potatoes
1 Spanish onion
2·5 cm (1 in) piece of fresh ginger root
25 g (1 oz) butter
1 teaspoon turmeric
1 teaspoon garam masala
1 dried chilli, crumbled
Generous 150 ml (¼ pint) yoghurt
225 g (8 oz) fresh, shelled or frozen peas
Salt and freshly ground black pepper
Chopped parsley, to garnish

Wipe the mushrooms over with a piece of dampened kitchen paper and trim the base of each stem; cut into six or eight wedges according to the size of the mushroom. Skin and slice the tomatoes. Scrub and cut the potatoes into sugar lump-sized cubes. Peel, halve and thinly slice the onion. Using a potato peeler, peel the ginger root and finely chop.

Heat the butter in a saucepan and gently fry the onion until softened and golden. Sprinkle in the fresh and dried spices, stir, then add about six tablespoons of yoghurt and the prepared mushrooms, cubed potatoes and peas. Bring to simmering point, cover and cook very gently for about 20 minutes or until the potatoes are just tender, stirring occasionally to check that the mixture is not catching on the base of the pan. Now uncover and simmer for another 5 minutes to reduce the sauce a little before spooning in a further 3–4 tablespoons of yoghurt, just enough to marble the curry. Sprinkle with chopped parsley and heat to a serveable temperature. Taste, season with salt and freshly ground black pepper and serve hot.

Vegetarian Burgers (*Makes 6*)

These are very easy to make. It is just the preliminary chopping, grating and grinding that takes some time, but once you have tried the burgers I am certain you will be very prepared to go through all the labours again.

2 medium carrots
2 stalks celery plus any leaves
1 medium onion
2 cabbage leaves
2 tablespoons brown breadcrumbs
50 g (2 oz) ground hazelnuts
2 tablespoons wheatgerm
½ teaspoon dried basil
1 standard (No. 4) egg
1 tablespoon tomato paste
1 tablespoon yoghurt
Salt and freshly ground black pepper

To coat:
Fine dry breadcrumbs and beaten egg
Oil, for brushing

Prepare the vegetables, peeling or scrubbing as required. Coarsely grate the carrots into a bowl and follow this with the very finely chopped celery, onion, and cabbage. Add the breadcrumbs, hazelnuts, wheatgerm and basil.

In a separate bowl, whisk together the egg, tomato paste and yoghurt. Add to the vegetable mixture. Mix well and taste and season with salt and freshly ground black pepper. Form the mix into six individual burgers, put on a plate, cover and chill for a few hours in the fridge.

Pre-heat the oven to 190 °C (350 °F/mark 4).

Dip each patty into beaten egg, then in breadcrumbs and place on an oiled baking sheet. Brush with oil and bake for 15 minutes. Turn carefully and bake for a further 15 minutes.

I usually serve these with a home-made tomato sauce or yoghurt on a bed of creamed cabbage with caraway and apple (page 169).

Nut and Mushroom Rissoles   (*Serves 4*)

The cliché food for vegetarians, referred to witheringly by
some meat-eaters who have obviously never tried them in
their lives or they would speak of them with considerably more
respect.

175 g (6 oz) stale, crustless wholemeal bread
Milk, stock or water
225 g (8 oz) mushrooms
1 onion
75 g (3 oz) cashew nuts
75 g (3 oz) hazelnut kernels
2 tablespoons oil
10 g ($\frac{1}{2}$ oz) butter
50 g (2 oz) bran
Rind and juice of 1 small lemon
Salt and freshly ground black pepper
1 egg, beaten
About 50 g (2 oz) dry fine brown breadcrumbs
Oil for shallow frying

Break the bread into small pieces and leave to soak in milk,
stock or water. Wipe, trim and finely chop the mushrooms;
peel and finely chop the onion. Mill the cashews and hazelnuts
into a bowl.

Heat the oil and butter in a medium saucepan and stir in the
onion. Cook until softened and golden. Add the mushrooms
and cook over a fairly high heat until all the excess liquid has
evaporated and the vegetables have formed a paste-like
consistency. Add this to the milled nuts with the squeezed-out
and shredded pieces of bread and the bran. Grate in the lemon
rind, beat thoroughly, taste and season with the lemon juice,
salt and freshly ground black pepper. Form the mixture into
round patties and chill until just before cooking.

Dip the patties briefly in beaten egg then coat in the breadcrumbs.

Heat enough oil in a frying pan to come halfway up the sides
of the patties. Fry on each side until golden and drain on
kitchen paper.

Serve with a home-made tomato sauce, or a yoghurt sauce made by adding a few snipped chives, a little crushed garlic and a squeeze of lemon juice to some natural yoghurt.

Greek Style Stuffed Tomatoes   (*Serves 6*)

A very simple but tasty recipe that could be a supper dish or starter. As a supper dish I usually serve it with a cold rice salad and bread. To make it more special, for a dinner party starter, I serve each tomato accompanied by small triangles of brown bread crisply fried in oil which has had a slightly crushed garlic clove marinated in it. Garnish by pushing a large sprig of parsley through the stalk part of each tomato 'lid'.

6 large tomatoes
900 g (2 lb) spinach
1 onion
About 4 tablespoons olive oil
40 g (1½ oz) pine nuts
Juice of ½ lemon
1 heaped teaspoon drained capers
2 cloves garlic, crushed
Salt and freshly ground black pepper

Pre-heat the oven to 180 °C (350 °F/mark 4)

Prepare the tomatoes by slicing off a thin 'cap' from the stalk end of each tomato. Scoop out the flesh using a teaspoon (sometimes a grapefruit knife is useful). Invert the tomatoes on a double sheet of kitchen paper and leave to drain. Wash the spinach thoroughly in cold water and discard the thick stalks and any damaged leaves. Drain and place the leaves in a large saucepan. Cover and cook over a fairly high heat, stirring frequently until all the leaves are just wilted and no more. Drain in a colander and when cool enough to handle, squeeze out any remaining water. Chop the spinach finely and transfer to a bowl.

142

Peel and finely chop the onion. Heat 2 tablespoons of oil in medium saucepan and cook the onion until softened and golden. Sprinkle in the pine nuts and allow these to lightly colour before removing the pan from the heat and transferring the contents to the bowl containing the spinach. Add the lemon juice, capers and crushed garlic. Mix well, then taste and season with salt and freshly ground black pepper.

Sit the tomatoes, cut side up, in an oiled baking dish and fill with the spinach mixture. Drizzle a little additional olive oil over each tomato and top with a 'lid.'

Bake in the centre of the oven for 30 minutes or until the tomatoes seem tender when tested with a thin skewer. Baste the tomatoes once or twice during baking with the juices that accumulate in the baking dish. As with all things Greek, serve at room temperature.

Watercress and Mushroom Roulade with Sour Cream Sauce

(Serves 4–6)

Please try not to be put off by the apparent length of this recipe. The results are more than worth it, in both taste and appearance. Ideal for a vegetarian dinner party, the number of servings depends very much on the accompaniments and number of courses you plan around this dish.

Filling:
2 smallish onions
450 g (1 lb) mushrooms
1 tablespoon oil
25 g (1 oz) butter
Rind of 1 small lemon, finely grated
1 small clove garlic, crushed
A squeeze of lemon juice
Salt and freshly ground black pepper
Freshly grated nutmeg

Roulade:
2 bunches watercress
50 g (2 oz) white mild cheese (Wensleydale, Lancashire, Caerphilly, etc.)
75 g (3 oz) plain, unbleached flour
275 ml (½ pint) milk
4 standard (No. 4) egg yolks
6 standard (No. 4) egg whites

Sauce:
50 g (2 oz) butter
2 teaspoons lemon juice
2 standard (No. 4) egg yolks
4 tablespoons soured cream
1 tablespoon dry Madeira or medium sherry

Garnish:
3 or 4 sprigs of watercress

Prepare the filling by peeling and chopping the onions very finely. Trim and wipe the mushrooms and chop them very finely too. Heat the oil and butter in a large saucepan and gently fry the onion for about 10 minutes, until just softened but not coloured. Stir in the mushrooms, lemon rind and garlic and cook gently for about a further 10–15 minutes, until all the excess liquid has evaporated and you are left with a spread-able paste. Taste and flavour with a squeeze of lemon juice, some salt and freshly ground black pepper and freshly grated nutmeg, and put aside.

Pre-heat the oven to 190 °C (375 °F/mark 5).

Line a large swiss roll tin, 33 × 23 cm (13 × 9 in) with foil to come up about 2·5 cm (1 in) above the sides of the tin. Brush the foil with melted butter and dust with flour.

Rinse the watercress thoroughly in cold water and discard all the coarse stalks and damaged leaves. Dry the remainder on kitchen paper, then chop finely. Grate the cheese.

To make the roulade, put the flour in a medium pan and gradually blend in the milk. Heat, stirring quickly with a balloon whisk. When the mixture looks alarmingly lumpy take the pan from the heat and beat until smooth. Now beat in the egg yolks and some nutmeg, salt and freshly ground black pepper.

In a separate, large, grease-free bowl, whisk the egg whites until stiff but not dry, and stir a quarter into the roulade mix. Now add the roulade mix to the egg whites with the cheese and watercress and fold everything together carefully. Spread the mixture in the prepared tin and bake in the centre of the oven for 18–20 minutes or until puffed and lightly tanned.

Meanwhile, have the mushroom filling warming gently and make the sauce. Melt, and only melt, the butter in a small saucepan. Whisk in the lemon juice, egg yolks and soured cream. Continue whisking and heating until the sauce thickens to a thin custard consistency. Do not let it boil or the sauce will curdle. And the Madeira or sherry, taste and season. Take off the heat but keep warm.

Have ready a clean tea towel dampened in hot water and spread out on a flat surface. Invert the swiss roll tin and turn the roulade out directly on to the tea towel. Peel off the foil and spread the roulade evenly all over with the mushroom mixture. Roll up, swiss roll style, from one long side to the other, and transfer to a warmed serving dish. Pour the sauce over, garnish with a few sprigs of watercress and serve hot.

Felafel

This mixture needs reducing to as smooth a paste as possible and an electric food chopper is the most efficient piece of equipment to do this. Otherwise, put the cooked chick peas through a food mill or mash them very thoroughly and then add the grated onion, finely chopped parsley, garlic and all the flavouring ingredients.

225 g (8 oz) chick peas
1 onion
2 cloves garlic
50 g (2 oz) parsley
1 teaspoon ground cummin
1 teaspoon ground coriander
½ teaspoon baking powder
¼ teaspoon cayenne pepper
Salt
Oil, for frying
Yoghurt, to serve

Put the chick peas in a saucepan with plenty of cold water to cover. Bring to the boil. Boil for 2 or 3 minutes, then remove the pan from the heat, cover and leave aside for a minimum of 1 hour but preferably about 3. Bring back to the boil once more. Cover and simmer gently for about 45 minutes, or until the chick peas are absolutely tender—try nibbling 2 or 3 to make absolutely sure—then drain in a colander.

Peel and coarsely chop the onion and garlic. Rinse the parsley under cold running water and pat dry with kitchen paper. Discard the stalks and chop the parsley. Put the drained chick peas, onion, garlic and parsley into an electric food chopper with the baking powder and the remaining flavouring ingredients and reduce to a paste. Form the mixture into little flattened rounds, about 4 cm (1½ in) diameter and ½ cm (¼ in) thick.

Fry them in just enough oil to coat the base of a frying pan. Serve with yoghurt.

Samosas

These are little cornet-shaped, deep-fried pasties, filled with a hottish, spicy mixture of peas, onion and potatoes. They are a little bit fiddly to prepare but well worth it, and make a delightful snack or stop-gap by using up left-overs. Any combination of cooked vegetables can be used in place of the peas; crisply cooked cabbage is particularly good.

Pastry:
225 g (8 oz) wholewheat flour
Generous pinch of salt
50 g (2 oz) butter

Filling:
1 onion
1 fresh chilli
About 275 g (10 oz) cooked potatoes
50 g (2 oz) butter
2 teaspoons peeled and finely chopped fresh ginger
175 g (6 oz) peas
¼ teaspoon chilli powder
1 teaspoon garam masala
1 teaspoon crushed coriander seeds
2 teaspoons lemon juice
Salt and freshly ground black pepper
Oil, for frying

Prepare the pastry by rubbing the butter into the flour and salt until the mixture resembles fine breadcrumbs. Gradually add sufficient water to form a firm dough; a scant 150 ml (¼ pint) is usually sufficient. Turn the dough out on to a lightly-floured surface and knead for 10 minutes. Leave it to rest on the work top, covered by an up-turned bowl, for about 30 minutes.

Meanwhile, prepare the filling. Peel and finely chop the onion, halve, de-seed and finely chop the chilli and chop the cooked potatoes. Melt the butter in a frying pan and stir in the onion, chilli and fresh ginger. Fry for 2 or 3 minutes. Stir in the remaining ingredients and 4 tablespoons of water. Cover and cook gently for 10 minutes. Uncover, taste and add more seasoning if needed. Remove the pan from the heat to allow the filling to cool.

Divide the dough into 12 sections and roll each piece into a ball. Keep the rest of the dough covered with a cloth while you roll out each ball to a round about 14 cm (5½ in) diameter. Cut each circle in half and brush the edges sparingly with water. Put a little filling on one half of each semi-circle and fold the other half of the semi-circle over the top to form a little cornet; pinch the edges together to seal. When all the samosas are ready, deep-fry them in oil at 190 °C (375 °F) for 2 or 3 minutes or until a good nut brown. Drain on kitchen paper. Keep hot in a single layer in the oven, if you like. Obviously they are crispy if served soon after being fried, but I like them when they are cold and, frankly, a bit 'wangy'.

For Indian food devotees these are nice served with a fresh coriander chutney.

Vegetable Cous Cous (Serves 6)

A lengthy-looking recipe, I know, but one that is easily and quickly prepared because the vegetables can be chopped while the cous cous is being initially cooked.

And to ward off your next question, cous cous is a type of fine semolina made from wheatgrain that has been ground and coated with a film of fine flour. This keeps each grain separate once it is cooked and makes it look a little like damp bread-crumbs. All I can say is that it is *dynamic* damp breadcrumbs and the finished dish is sensational when it comes to the table. You will need your largest oval meat dish. The cous cous is piled around the edge and the vegetables heaped up in the centre. The whole is topped off by a spicy, fiery tomato sauce and served with a creamy home-made yoghurt.

Cous Cous:

450 g (1 lb) prepared cous cous
25 g (1 oz) butter
2 tablespoons olive oil
1 teaspoon salt
Freshly ground black pepper

Vegetable Mixture:

3 medium carrots
1 large green pepper
2 medium onions
3 celery stalks
110 g (4 oz) button mushrooms
4 tomatoes
3 courgettes
225 g (8 oz) broccoli florets
110 g (4 oz) peas, frozen or fresh
110 g (4 oz) broad beans, frozen or fresh
1 scant litre (1½ pints) vegetable stock
110 g (4 oz) chick peas, cooked
2 fat cloves garlic, crushed

Sauce:

2 tablespoons tomato paste
1 dessertspoon paprika
¼ teaspoon chilli powder (more or less to taste)
1 teaspoon ground cummin
1 teaspoon coriander
Plenty of chopped parsley, to garnish

Put the cous cous in a large mixing bowl and gradually work in 8 tablespoons of water, running the grain through the finger-tips as though rubbing fat into flour. Line a colander with a clean tea towel wrung out in hot water and select a saucepan over which the colander will fit snugly. Bring about 2·5 cm (1 in) of water to the boil in the pan. When you turn your attention once again to the cous cous, the grains will have 'set' together, so separate them by using the same 'rubbing in' technique as before, then transfer the grain to the cloth-lined colander. Lightly fold the edges of the cloth over the grain and steam for 30 minutes. Check that the water neither boils away, nor is in contact with the grain during cooking, and rake through the grains occasionally with a fork to keep them separate.

Meanwhile prepare the vegetables. Scrub the carrots, top and tail and cut into rings no thicker than 1 cm ($\frac{1}{2}$ in). Halve and de-seed the pepper and cut into postage-stamp pieces. The onions can be peeled and cut into 6 wedges each and the celery scrubbed and cut into squares similar to that of the green pepper. Have all these vegetables ready in one bowl as they will need slightly longer cooking than the remaining ones. Of these, the mushrooms need wiping over with kitchen paper and the base of each stalk trimmed slightly. Peel the tomatoes, either by immersing them in boiling water for a few seconds or by skewering them with a fork and holding them over a gas flame; leave them whole. Wipe, top, tail and cut the courgettes into 1-cm ($\frac{1}{2}$ in) thick slices. Separate the broccoli florets into tiny heads, no bigger than a $\frac{1}{2}$ pence piece. Put all these vegetables ready in a separate bowl with the peas and beans (if these are fresh then add them to the first batch of vegetables).

When the cous cous has steamed for 30 minutes, transfer it to a heatproof bowl and gradually work in a further 8 table-spoons of water, followed by the butter; oil and seasoning. Use a wooden spoon or fork at this stage, as it will be too hot for hands. Return the bowl to steam over the simmering water and cover lightly with the folded tea cloth. Cook for a further 30 minutes, occasionally forking through the grains.

Meanwhile, heat the stock in a large saucepan. When boiling, tip in the first bowl of vegetables and add the cooked chick peas, crushed garlic and a little salt and freshly ground black pepper. Bring to boiling point, cover and simmer gently for 10 minutes.

Have the oven and plates warming on the lowest setting.

After 10 minutes tip the second bowl of vegetables into the stock, stir, bring to simmering point once more, then cover and cook for a further 5 minutes.

As soon as the cous cous is cooked, transfer it from the bowl on to the warmed oval meat dish and spread it out around the edge of the dish to form a retaining wall for the vegetables. Using a large draining spoon, remove the cooked vegetables from the hot stock and heap up in the centre of the serving dish, then return it to the oven to keep warm.

Now in a bowl blend the sauce ingredients together with a little of the remaining hot vegetable liquor, stir into the rest and boil briskly until the sauce has reduced by about a third and has a good, thin consistency. Taste and adjust the chilli heat of the sauce to your requirements. Spoon half of this over the vegetables, sprinkle thickly with chopped parsley and serve immediately accompanied by a bowl of the remaining sauce and a bowl of yoghurt.

NON-VEGETARIAN DISHES

Roast Chicken with Brown Rice Stuffing
(Serves 6)

This recipe uses every part of the bird in an effort to maximise the flavour so often lacking in the chickens we buy nowadays. Buy undressed, fresh poultry whenever you can and have the poulterer or butcher dress it for you on the spot. Make the most of this opportunity now because if Common Market rulings are applied here it will soon be illegal to sell undressed poultry.

A 2 kg (4 lb) (dressed weight) fresh chicken, with giblets
Squeeze of lemon juice
Salt and freshly ground black pepper
50 g (2 oz) soft butter
1 large Spanish onion
75 g (3 oz) blanched, halved almonds
2 mugs brown rice
50 g (2 oz) currants
1 teaspoon dried thyme
4 mugs boiling stock or water

Remove the giblets and fat from the body cavity of the bird and season its interior with lemon juice, salt and freshly ground black pepper. Transfer to a roasting tin and smear the bird all over with butter.

Coarsely cut up the liver, heart and gizzard of the bird. Peel and chop the onion. Heat the chicken fat in a large saucepan until it has reduced enough to give about 2 tablespoons of liquid fat. Discard the shrivelled pieces, stir in the chopped onion and cook until softened and pale golden. Turn up the heat and add the chopped giblets and almonds. Cook, stirring frequently, until nicely browned. Add the rice and turn to coat the grains in the fat before adding the currants, thyme and boiling stock or water. Bury the chicken neck down in the rice mixture, return to simmering point, then cover and simmer gently for about 40 minutes, until the rice is *just* tender. If all the liquid has not been absorbed by this stage, uncover and turn up the heat to evaporate the excess. Taste and season the rice with salt and freshly ground black pepper. Remove the pan from the heat, discard the chicken neck, cover and leave to cool for 10 minutes.

Meanwhile, pre-heat the oven to 200 °C (400 °F/mark 6).

Fill the body cavity of the chicken with about one-third of the rice mixture; it doesn't matter at all that the rice is still hot. Put the chicken in the oven and roast for 1–1¼ hours, basting occasionally. Keep the rice warm in the covered pan while the chicken cooks.

When ready to serve, remove the chicken to a warmed serving dish and surround with the rice from the pan. Cover and keep hot while you make a gravy with the pan juices in the usual way. Serve hot with gravy.

Wholewheat Chicken Liver Gougère   (*Serves 4–5*)

This recipe follows the general theme in this section of making a little meat go a long way. It re-heats quite happily.

Wholewheat Choux Paste:
275 ml (½ pint) water
85 g (3½ oz) butter
125 g (4½ oz) strong brown flour
110 g (4 oz) Cheddar cheese
3 standard (No. 4) eggs
½ teaspoon marjoram
Salt and freshly ground black pepper
Grated nutmeg

Filling:
1 onion
110 g (4 oz) button mushrooms
25 g (1 oz) butter
225 g (8 oz) chicken livers
1 tablespoon wholewheat flour
396 g (14 oz) tin tomatoes
2 teaspoons tomato paste
Salt and freshly ground black pepper
1 tablespoon parsley, chopped

Pre-heat the oven to 200 °C (400 °F/mark 6)

Start by making the choux paste. Put the water and butter in a medium saucepan and bring to the boil. As soon as the water boils and the fat has melted, shoot in all the flour in one go and stir vigorously. In a few minutes the mixture will have formed a soft ball around the spoon. Remove the pan from the heat and leave the mixture to cool while you grate the cheese.

Break the eggs into the mix and beat them in, one at a time. Beat in the flavourings and all but 25 g (1 oz) of grated cheese. Set the mixture aside and prepare the filling.

Peel and chop the onion; wipe, trim and thinly slice the mushrooms.

Heat the butter in a saucepan and briskly fry the chicken

livers for 3 or 4 minutes. Drain and remove to a plate. Fry the onion in the fat remaining in the pan until softened and golden. Add the sliced mushrooms, cook for a minute or two, then stir in the flour. Cook for a further minute before adding the tomatoes. Stir and leave to simmer uncovered for about 15 minutes or until reduced to a sauce-like consistency. Remove the pan from the heat. Stir in the chicken livers and any juices. Add the tomato paste and taste and season with salt and freshly ground black pepper.

Butter a dish about $25 \times 15 \times 6\frac{1}{2}$ cm, ($10 \times 6 \times 2\frac{1}{2}$ in).

Spoon the choux paste into the dish to form an even band around the inside edge. Pour the chicken liver filling into the centre and sprinkle the remaining choux paste with the reserved grated cheese over the top.

Bake in the top half of the oven for 40 minutes or until the choux paste is well risen, browned and crisp. Serve hot, sprinkled with the chopped parsley.

Curried Lamb with Chick Peas   (*Serves 5–6*)

The ghee referred to in the recipe is clarified butter or margarine and both types are available in tins from specialist Indian or delicatessen shops. As it is very useful to have in the kitchen, you may like to make your own. Simply put either butter or margarine in a pan and simmer for about an hour. Strain and store in a covered jar and you will have a useful non-browning medium in which to fry all manner of foods.

175 g (6 oz) chick peas, soaked overnight
900 g (2 lb) boned shoulder of lamb
1 aubergine, about 350 g (12 oz)
450 g (1 lb) tomatoes
3 fresh chillies
6 tablespoons ghee
1 teaspoon turmeric
1 teaspoon garam masala
2 garlic cloves, crushed
1 tablespoon peeled and finely chopped fresh ginger
2 tablespoons chopped fresh mint
150 ml (¼ pint) yoghurt
1 large onion
Coarsely chopped parsley, to garnish

Drain the chick peas and transfer to a saucepan with plenty of fresh, cold water. Bring to the boil, cover and boil gently for about 1 hour, or until the peas are absolutely tender.

Meanwhile, cut the meat into 2·5 cm (1 in) cubes, discarding any excess fat. Discard the stalk end from the aubergine, wipe and cut into sugarcube-sized pieces. Peel and thickly slice the tomatoes. Cut the chillies in half lengthways and rinse away the seeds under the tap, then slice the pods up very finely.

Heat 3 tablespoons of the ghee in a large saucepan. Fry the meat, a small batch at a time, over a high heat until browned. As it browns, use a draining spoon to remove it to a plate. When all the meat has been browned stir the aubergine into the pan and fry until coloured before adding the turmeric and garam masala. Cook for a minute or two, then add the tomatoes, chillies, crushed garlic, ginger and mint. Return the meat to the pan with the drained chick peas and 425 ml ($\frac{3}{4}$ pint) of their cooking liquor. Bring to simmering point, cover and cook gently for 15 minutes, then uncover and continue cooking for about $1\frac{1}{4}$ hours, or until the meat is absolutely tender and has a thick sauce. Stir in the yoghurt and cook for a further 10 minutes.

Just before serving, peel, halve and thinly slice the onion. Heat the remaining ghee in a separate pan. Stir in the onion and cook over a moderate heat until it is golden brown and crispy. Remove and drain on kitchen paper before forking about three quarters of it into the meat mixture. Use the rest as a garnish with the chopped parsley. Serve hot.

Curried Beef and Beans (*Serves 4–6*)

This recipe is an extension of the usual chilli con carne and is the only recipe in which I have used coconut. This is not an ingredient I would use normally but, without it, the flavour of this dish is incomplete. If fresh coconut seems too much like hard work, use the packet desiccated variety.

900 g (2 lb) braising steak
2 medium onions
25 g (1 oz) ghee or clarified butter
1 tablespoon coriander seeds
1 teaspoon poppy seeds
4 cardamom pods
5 cm (2 in) stick cinnamon
5 cloves
1 teaspoon cummin seeds
3-4 large dried chillies
1 teaspoon turmeric powder
2 fat cloves garlic, peeled
25 g (1 oz) piece fresh peeled ginger root
225 g (8 oz) red kidney beans, soaked overnight
4 tablespoons fresh grated coconut
Juice of ½ lemon
Salt

Trim and cut the beef into small pieces, about the size of your small fingernail. Peel and chop the onions to a roughly comparable size.

Heat the butter in a large pan and fry the onion until golden. Add the meat, a small amount at a time, and allow it to colour before pushing it to the side of the pan to make room for the next batch. While the meat is frying, put the coriander, poppy seeds and cardamoms in a mortar and crush. Add this to the browned beef and onions, together with the cinnamon stick, cloves, cummin seeds, crumbled dried chillies and turmeric. Stir and leave to cook for a few minutes, while you combine 570 ml (1 pint) water with the garlic and ginger in the goblet of a liquidiser. Blend until no obvious lumps remain and pour into the pan. Stir in the drained beans, cover and simmer gently for 1 hour. Uncover and stir in the grated coconut and continue to cook very gently, uncovered, for a further hour or until both meat and beans are tender and enough of the liquid has evaporated to give a good sauce consistency. Taste and add the lemon juice and salt as required. Serve with rice. It is also good served with mounds of spinach and, of course, yoghurt.

Savoury Crumble

(*Serves 5–6*)

The combination of vegetables and crumble topping makes it possible to feed the maximum number of people on the minimum of meat. And if you have never tried this type of savoury topping, *do*! It is very good.

Mince Base:
1 Spanish onion
2 smallish turnips
3 medium carrots
2 large celery stalks
2 tablespoons oil
450 g (1 lb) minced beef
397 g (14 oz) tin tomatoes
1–2 teaspoons tomato paste
1 teaspoon mixed dried herbs
1 bayleaf
425 ml (¾ pint) beef stock
Salt and freshly ground black pepper

Crumble Topping:
175 g (6 oz) wholewheat flour
50 g (2 oz) grated Parmesan cheese
25 g (1 oz) wheatgerm
½ teaspoon mixed herbs
110 g (4 oz) butter

Peel and dice the onion, and the turnips. Scrub and dice the carrots and celery stalks.

Heat the oil in a medium saucepan and gently fry the prepared vegetables until softened and golden. Turn the heat up high and add the minced meat, a little at a time. When the mince has browned, lower the heat and add the tomatoes, tomato paste, herbs and stock. Season and simmer gently, uncovered, for 1–1¼ hours, stirring occasionally. Aim to have the consistency of the mince mixture a little on the wet side to counteract the dryness of the crumble topping. Taste and season the mince with salt and freshly ground black pepper if necessary, then transfer to a deep baking dish.

Pre-heat the oven to 180 °C (350 °F/mark 4).

To make the crumble topping put all the dry ingredients together in a bowl and rub the butter into them until the mixture is like dry breadcrumbs. Season with salt and freshly ground black pepper and sprinkle evenly over the surface of the mince. Bake for 40 minutes or until the crumble is nicely browned and the mince piping hot. Serve with mounds of lightly boiled, buttery cabbage.

Bacon and Lentil Casserole (*Serves 6*)

This method of cooking the bacon joint is for when you have no time to soak it overnight. If you are organised and have already done so then ignore the preliminary boiling up.

1 kg 125 g (2½ lb) collar of bacon
1 large onion
2 turnips, small apple size
2 large carrots
3 celery stalks
2 tablespoons oil
25 g (1 oz) butter
397 g (14 oz) tin tomatoes
1 clove garlic, crushed
½ teaspoon dried thyme
¼ teaspoon dried sage
1 bayleaf
225 g (8 oz) green lentils
1 tablespoon tomato paste
Salt and freshly ground black pepper

Put the bacon joint in a saucepan and cover with cold water. Bring to the boil, then drain it off and replace with fresh water. Bring to the boil once more, then simmer gently for 35 minutes. When the time is up, hoist the bacon out, keeping the cooking liquor, and leave the joint to cool a little before stripping off the strings and rind. Cut the bacon into 2·5 cm (1 in) cubes, discarding any excess fat or gristle. Cover and put aside.

Meanwhile, peel and cube the onion and turnips; scrub and dice the carrots and celery.

Heat the oil and butter in a large casserole and stir in the prepared vegetables. Fry gently over a low heat for about 10 minutes, until they are softened and golden. Measure out 570 ml (1 pint) of the reserved bacon stock and add to the casserole with the tomatoes, the garlic, herbs and cubed bacon. Pick the lentils over carefully, transfer to a sieve and sluice with cold water; drain and stir into the casserole. Bring to simmering point, cover and cook gently for 45 minutes. Uncover, stir in the tomato paste and continue to simmer for a further 15 minutes. Taste and check that everything is tender. Season with freshly ground black pepper; it probably will not need more salt. Serve hot.

Savoury Stuffed Apples (*Serves 4*)

Hollowing out fruit and vegetables can be a bit tricky but, as with the apples in this recipe, the combination of a grapefruit knife and teaspoon seems the best way. Try to rid yourself of the idea that stuffed apples are strictly for dessert. They work very well stuffed with sausagemeat and are delicious.

4 cooking apples
1 onion
110 g (4 oz) button mushrooms
40 g (1½ oz) butter
225 g (8 oz) sausagemeat
50 g (2 oz) fresh brown breadcrumbs
½ teaspoon crumbled rosemary
Salt and freshly ground black pepper
About 25 g (1 oz) butter
150 ml (¼ pint) dry cider
1 teaspoon cider vinegar

Pre-heat the oven to 180 °C (350 °F/mark 4)

Cut a 'cap' from the stalk end of each apple in the shape of an inverted cone and reserve. Hollow out the fruit leaving a 1 cm (½ in) thick wall. Discard the sections of core but reserve and chop the rest. Keep the base intact. Peel and finely chop the onion. Trim the mushroom stems and wipe each one over with a section of damp kitchen paper, then chop them finely.

In a frying pan, heat the butter and stir in the onion. Cook until softened and golden before stirring in the mushrooms, then, after 3 or 4 minutes, stir in the sausagemeat. Continue cooking, mashing down the sausagemeat until the mixture is a uniform crumble. Add the chopped apple, breadcrumbs and rosemary; taste and season with salt and freshly ground black pepper.

Select a deep, lidded baking dish that will just take the apples nicely. Spoon the filling into the fruit (it does not matter too much if some of it goes overboard) and dot the top of each one with a knob of butter. Replace the 'caps' and pour in the cider and cider vinegar. Cover with the lid and bake for 45 minutes or until the apples seem tender when tested with a thin skewer, but don't let them disintegrate. Serve immediately with the baking juices spooned over.

Stuffed Cabbage Leaves   (*Serves* 5–6)

900 g–1 kg 350 g (2–3 lb) head of green cabbage, cleaned
Salt and freshly ground black pepper

Stuffing:
1 onion
10 g (½ oz) butter
1 tablespoon oil
450 g (1 lb) minced pork
50 g (2 oz) cooked brown rice
1 clove garlic, crushed
2 eggs
2 tablespoons paprika
¼ teaspoon dried marjoram

Sauce:
397 g (14 oz) tin tomatoes
150 ml (¼ pint) chicken stock
2–3 tablespoons soured cream

Bring a large saucepan of salted water to the boil and place the cleaned cabbage in the pan, stalk end up. Bring back to the boil and simmer for about 8 minutes, then hoist the cabbage out and leave to cool. Working with the cabbage still stalk end up, cut the large, outer leaves from the main stalk and peel them off one by one. You will need about 15 leaves in all. Pat the leaves dry on kitchen paper.

To prepare the stuffing, start by peeling and chopping the onion. Heat the butter and oil together in a medium saucepan and fry gently until the onion is softened and golden.

Put the minced pork in a bowl, add the onion and garlic and the remaining stuffing ingredients. Season well with salt and freshly ground black pepper.

Make a V-shaped cut to remove the thickest part of the stalk from the base of each leaf, place about one tablespoon of stuffing in the centre of each leaf, fold in the sides and roll the leaf up tightly. Pack the rolled leaves closely in a casserole and pour over the contents of the tin of tomatoes and the stock. Cover and cook gently over a low heat for 1–1¼ hours.

Carefully drain and remove the cabbage rolls to a serving dish and boil up the remaining pan juices until reduced by about a third. Turn down the heat and stir in the soured cream. Taste, season and pour the sauce over the rolls. Serve hot.

VEGETABLES

In this chapter I have aimed for the type of vegetable that will readily make the transition from an accompaniment, to a main-meal dish suitable for a family supper. For most of these recipes the simple addition of ingredients like eggs, bread, a cheese sauce or bacon rolls can turn them into more substantial and cheap main meals.

I was greatly tempted at the outset to give very basic recipes for cooking fresh vegetables, so that people could enjoy their maximum natural flavour. But on reflection this did not seem to offer the reader enough, quite literally, to get his teeth into, so in the recipe introductions I have suggested variations suitable for any occasion.

It is a pity, though, that we British are so bad with vegetables. I am afraid we rightly deserve the dreadful criticisms we have received for them in the past, but I think we are gradually realising that fresh young vegetables should be cooked, but only just, and served immediately. Catching on, too, is the French idea that these dishes are worthy of standing alone as a course in their own right.

Steaming vegetables is also catching on, so try it if you have not already done so. Steam new potatoes in their skins over water infused with fresh herbs. Carrots, courgettes, cauli-flowers and brussels sprouts all take very kindly to this treatment, and if you have a glut of peas in the garden, steam them in their pods for about 15 minutes and serve like asparagus with plenty of seasoned, melted butter poured all over. Eat with your fingers by opening the pods and immediately shooting the juices and peas into your mouth: messy but delicious. Baking vegetables in their jackets can be explored a bit further too: potatoes of course, but try onions or beetroots this way—they are excellent.

One further comment is that whenever and wherever possible, avoid peeling vegetables. Their flavour is often so much better when the skins are left intact. It is quite enough merely to scrub them well.

BABYCHAM
TEL: SHEPTON MALLET 3333

Cabbage with Cream, Caraway and Apple

(*Serves 4–6*)

Delicious either by itself or with light meat dishes such as pork, veal, rabbit or pies, and also some quiches.

450 g (1 lb) green cabbage
1 large onion
1 large cooking apple
25 g (1 oz) butter
1 teaspoon black peppercorns
½ teaspoon rock salt
1 teaspoon caraway seeds
150 ml (¼ pint) soured cream

Rinse and shred the cabbage leaves; peel and chop the onion. Peel the cooking apple if you prefer (I never bother), core and finely chop.

Melt the butter in a large casserole or saucepan. Stir in the onion and cook over a low heat until softened and golden.

Meanwhile, put the peppercorns and rock salt into a mortar and crush. Add the caraway seeds and simply bruise them (don't crush or pulverise them) and stir into the onion. Add the apple, cook for a minute, then stir in the prepared cabbage. Cover and cook gently for about 10 minutes, until the cabbage looks slightly softened and wilted. Stir in the cream, re-cover and continue to cook over a low heat for a further 20 minutes or until the cabbage is just cooked. Stir fairly frequently to check that the cabbage mixture is not catching on the base of the pan. Taste and adjust the seasoning if necessary, before serving. Serve hot.

Red Cabbage with Orange and Port

(Serves 5–6)

An alternative to the usual way of cooking red cabbage and a lot quicker. Serve with rich, wine-flavoured stews or the celebration kind of meats one usually eats around Christmas.

900 g (2 lb) red cabbage
1 onion
Rind and juice of 2 oranges
Juice of 1 lemon
1 clove garlic, crushed
1½ teaspoons caraway seeds
Salt and freshly ground black pepper
3 tablespoons redcurrant jelly (home-made if possible)
25 g (1 oz) butter
2 tablespoons ruby port

Discard the tough outer leaves of the cabbage, cut it into quarters and remove the hard stalk, then shred the cabbage finely. Transfer to a large saucepan or flameproof casserole.

Peel and chop the onion and add to the casserole. Use a zester to remove the rind from the oranges, otherwise peel them thinly with a potato peeler and cut the strips of zest into hair-like strips. Add to the casserole with the combined juices of the oranges and the lemon, the crushed garlic and caraway seeds. Season with salt and freshly ground black pepper and stir to mix thoroughly. Spoon the redcurrant jelly on top and add the butter, then cover and cook gently for 1 hour, giving the cabbage a good churn around from time to time to make sure it cooks evenly. When it is just tender and ready to serve, taste and add more seasoning if necessary. Stir in the port and serve piping hot.

Young Broad Beans in Curd Cheese Sauce   (*Serves 3–4*)

This is a way to serve broad beans in the pod but they must be picked very young, when they are scarcely more than finger thick. If you have never tried broad beans this way, you haven't lived!

450 g (1 lb) young broad beans in their pods

Sauce:
110 g (4 oz) curd cheese
2 egg yolks
1 tablespoon snipped chives
Squeeze of lemon juice
Salt and freshly ground black pepper

Top and tail the beans, rinse, drain and cut in 2·5 cm (1 in) lengths. Cook them in the minimum of boiling, salted water for about 8 minutes or until *just* tender. Drain the beans reserving the cooking liquid.

Quickly combine 150 ml (¼ pint) of the bean cooking liquid (made up with water if necessary) with the curd cheese and egg yolks in the goblet of a liquidiser. Blend until smooth and pour into the empty pan. Return the beans to the pan with the chives. Re-heat gently, stirring. Add the lemon juice, taste and season with salt and freshly ground black pepper. When the sauce has thickened sufficiently to coat the beans, serve instantly.

Cucumbers in Cider (*Serves 4-6*)

Not a vegetable that is usually cooked nowadays but was much more popular in our grandmother's time and, as usual, granny knew what she was about! A good way of dealing with a greenhouse glut.

2 cucumbers
1 Spanish onion
40 g (1½ oz) butter
150 ml (¼ pint) dry cider
1 dessertspoon each of wholewheat flour and butter
Salt and freshly ground black pepper

Wipe and trim the cucumbers top and bottom, then cut into sugarcube-size pieces. Peel, quarter and thinly slice the onion.

Melt the butter in a large saucepan and stir in the sliced onion. Cook over a gentle heat for about 5 minutes or until the onion is softened but not coloured. Stir in the cucumber and cook for a few minutes over a moderate heat before pouring in the cider. Cover and simmer gently for about 10 minutes or until the cucumber is cooked but retains a little bit of a crunch.

Meanwhile, work the butter and flour together to a paste in a small bowl. When the cucumber is cooked, turn off the heat and stir in small parts of the paste. Re-heat, stirring until the mixture thickens and boils gently for a couple of minutes. Taste and season with salt and freshly ground black pepper. Serve hot.

Braised Celery with Tomato and Coriander

(*Serves* 6)

6 young, small heads of celery
1 Spanish onion
450 g (1 lb) tomatoes
2–3 tablespoons oil
1 teaspoon sea salt
1 teaspoon coriander seeds
½ teaspoon black peppercorns
1 clove garlic, peeled
275 ml (½ pint) chicken or vegetable stock
1–2 teaspoons tomato paste
Squeeze of lemon juice
Chopped parsley, to garnish

Trim the celery heads so they are about 15 cm (6 in) long. Scrub, leaving them whole. Peel and finely chop the onion. Peel and thickly slice the tomatoes.

Bring a large pan of salted water to the boil and put the celery in (you will probably have to cook the celery in two batches). Bring the water back to the boil and simmer for 3 minutes. Remove the celery to a colander and sluice with cold water.

Heat enough oil to cover the base of a casserole that is large enough to take the celery heads in a single layer. Stir in the onion and cook gently until softened but not coloured.

Meanwhile, put the salt, coriander seeds, peppercorns and garlic in a mortar and crush together. Add the sliced tomatoes to the casserole, followed by the crushed flavourings. Stir and cook gently for a minute or two before adding the stock. Arrange the celery in the casserole, bring to simmering point, cover and cook slowly for 1¼–1½ hours or until the celery feels tender when tested with a thin skewer. Drain and remove the celery to a serving dish and keep hot. Boil the remaining pan juices briskly to reduce them to a sauce-like consistency. Add the tomato paste and lemon juice, taste and season again if necessary. Pour the sauce over the celery, sprinkle with chopped parsley and serve.

Green Tomatoes Provençal   *(Serves 4)*

Since I always seem to get left with a glut of green tomatoes
(mine never reach the ripened stage!), I had to find some way
of using them besides chutney. I am happy to report that you
can do everything with a green tomato that you do with a red
one, as long as it is cooked in the process.

2 rashers back bacon
1 dozen black olives
450 g (1 lb) green tomatoes
110 g (4 oz) soft brown breadcrumbs
2 rounded tablespoons chopped parsley
1 clove garlic, crushed
2 tablespoons olive oil
Salt and freshly ground black pepper

Pre-heat the oven to 200 °C (400 °F/mark 6)

Rind the bacon and cut the rashers across into striplets. Pit
and finely chop the olives. Wipe and cut the tomatoes in half.
Arrange them, cut side up, in a single layer in a shallow,
greased baking dish.

Put the breadcrumbs in a bowl and add the bacon, chopped
olives and remaining ingredients. Go easy on the salt though;
the bacon and olives contribute a fair amount. Toss the
ingredients together with a fork to mix lightly so it all stays
separate and does not go into a solid mass. Sprinkle over the
tomatoes, cover with foil and bake in the top half of the oven
for 20 minutes. Uncover and allow the topping to brown for a
further 10–15 minutes. Test with a sharp knife or thin skewer
to see if the tomatoes are done. Serve hot.

Delicious Baked Parsnips   (*Serves 4*)

Again, the sort of vegetable recipe which is so nice it is a dish on its own right.

900 g (2 lb) young parsnips
1 Spanish onion
25 g (1 oz) butter
2 tablespoons oil
2 tablespoons porridge oats
150 ml (¼ pint) soured cream
1 teaspoon French mustard
150 ml (¼ pint) vegetable or light chicken stock
Salt and freshly ground black pepper

Topping:
25 g (1 oz) mild Cheddar cheese, grated
2 tablespoons wheatgerm

Pre-heat the oven to 150 °C (300 °F/mark 3)

Prepare the parsnips by topping and tailing, and peeling if necessary. Cut in four lengthways and slice away the central woody section from each piece. Peel and chop the onion.

Heat the butter and oil together in a casserole. Add the prepared parsnips and onion to the pan and stir to coat with the fat. Cook gently for 10 minutes until golden. Sprinkle in the porridge oats, stir again and cook for a minute or two before stirring in the soured cream, mustard and then the stock. Season, cover and bake for 1–1¼ hours or until the parsnips seem tender when tested with a thin skewer. Check the consistency of the sauce; it should be nicely creamy. If it is at all sticky or stodgy then add a little more stock or water.

Combine the grated cheese and wheatgerm and sprinkle over the parsnips. Transfer to cook under the grill until well toasted. Serve hot.

Aubergines Baked with Mozzarella

(*Serves 4*)

This makes a good supper dish served very simply with a green salad and fresh brown bread.

2 large aubergines, about 275 g (10 oz) a piece
Salt and freshly ground black pepper
1 onion
About 3 tablespoons oil
1 clove garlic, crushed
1 tablespoon chopped fresh basil
110 g (4 oz) Mozzarella cheese
1 tablespoon drained capers, chopped
6 drained anchovy fillets, chopped
2 large tomatoes

Trim the green stalk end from each aubergine, wipe and slice in half. Use a grapefruit knife or a teaspoon to remove the pulp from the aubergine halves, leaving a shell not less than $\frac{1}{2}$ cm ($\frac{1}{4}$ in) thick. Sprinkle the shells liberally with salt and leave upside down to drain for about 45 minutes.

Meanwhile, chop the aubergine pulp. Peel and chop the onion.

Pre-heat the oven to 180 °C (350 °F/mark 4).

Heat 2 tablespoons of oil in a medium saucepan and gently fry the onion until softened and golden. Stir in the chopped pulp, crushed garlic and half the basil. Season with salt and freshly ground black pepper and cook over a low heat for about 10 minutes, stirring occasionally.

Wipe the aubergine shells with kitchen paper and arrange in a small, oiled roasting tin or baking dish. Spoon the pulp mixture into the shells, arrange about 3 slices of Mozzarella on top of each and sprinkle with the chopped capers and anchovies. Lastly, slice the tomatoes and arrange 4 or 5 slices on each shell. Sprinkle with the remaining basil and dribble a little additional olive oil over the lot (use some of the anchovy oil if you like). Season with salt and freshly ground black pepper and bake in the top half of the oven for 40 minutes. Serve hot.

Spiced Vegetable Mixture (*Serves 4–5*)

Again, this is a dish that can be a meal in its own right if served with brown rice and almonds. I have also discovered that spiced poppadums (which can be bought in most Indian shops or delicatessens now) crumbled over the top, make a rather different and welcome change. Served straight, as a side dish, it is best with omelettes or grilled fish steaks.

2 onions
2 large carrots
1 medium cauliflower
1 cooking apple
1 teaspoon cummin seeds
1 teaspoon coriander seeds
1 teaspoon mustard seeds
1 teaspoon rock salt
2 tablespoons oil
1 teaspoon turmeric
¼ teaspoon cayenne pepper
275 ml (½ pint) yoghurt

Peel and chop the onions. Top, tail and scrub the carrots, cut them in four lengthways, before slicing them across thinly. Divide the cauliflower into small florets, no bigger than a 5p coin; quarter, core and chop the apple.

Put the flavouring seeds and salt into a mortar and crush.

Heat the oil in a large saucepan and stir in the prepared vegetables and apple. Cook over a fairly high heat until lightly browned, then turn the heat down to low, add the pounded flavourings, turmeric, cayenne and yoghurt. Stir and bring to simmering point, then cover and cook gently for about 8–10 minutes or until the vegetables are just tender. Uncover and increase the heat to reduce the pan juices to a good sauce consistency. Serve hot.

Pan Haggerty

Simple but delicious. Good served with a green salad as a supper dish or to accompany grilled pork, grilled white fish or chicken.

700 g (1½ lb) potatoes
225 g (8 oz) onions
110 g–175 g (4–6 oz) cheese
25 g (1 oz) lard or dripping
Salt and freshly ground black pepper

Peel and thinly slice the potatoes about 3 mm (⅛ in) thick. Peel, halve and very thinly slice the onions and grate the cheese.

Melt the fat in a frying pan about 20–23 cm (8–9 in) in diameter and swirl around the pan to coat the edge. Use half the sliced potatoes to line the base and side of the pan. Combine the grated cheese, sliced onion and a little salt and freshly ground black pepper and put in the pan. Arrange the remaining potatoes over the top and season again. Cover the pan with a plate and cook over a low heat for about 40 minutes or until the potatoes are absolutely tender. Serve from the pan, cut in wedges.

Baked Potatoes with Juniper Butter Sauce

(*Serves 6*)

Because of the juniper flavouring, these jacket potatoes would go well with all manner of rich roasts, grills and gamey things; or just serve them on their own with a salad.

6 old potatoes

Sauce:
1 small onion
225 g (8 oz) butter
Juice of ½ lemon
2 cloves garlic
1 teaspoon juniper berries
1 teaspoon rock salt
½ teaspoon black peppercorns
2 rounded tablespoons chopped parsley, to garnish

Pre-heat the oven to 200 °C (400 °F/mark 6)

Scrub the potatoes very thoroughly with a stiff bristle brush and dry them on kitchen paper. Prick each potato once or twice with a fork and rub with a buttered paper. Bake in the oven for 1–1¼ hours or until the potatoes feel tender when squeezed.

Meanwhile, peel and finely chop the onion. Melt the butter in a small saucepan with the lemon juice. Add the onion and simmer gently for 3 or 4 minutes. While the onion is softening, crush the garlic, juniper berries, rock salt and peppercorns together in a pestle and mortar. Add the crushed flavourings to the butter and pull the pan aside from the heat. Cover and leave the flavours to develop while the potatoes bake.

To serve, put a baked potato on each heated serving plate, cut a cross in the top of each and gently squeeze the sides in to open up the gash. Re-heat the butter sauce until bubbling and spoon about 2 tablespoons of it into each potato. Sprinkle thickly with the parsley and add a further 2 tablespoons of butter sauce to each potato. Serve hot.

Aïoli with Baked Potatoes (*Serves 6*)

A quick garlic-flavoured mayonnaise done in a liquidiser. It is not only good with baked potatoes but also as a full-blown meal, garnishing a serving dish full of cooked vegetables like cauliflower, broccoli, leeks, carrots and accompanied by good home-made brown bread. Enhances the plainest of white fish too!

6 old potatoes

Aïoli:
2 standard (No. 4) eggs
4 garlic cloves, peeled
1 teaspoon Dijon mustard
1 tablespoon tarragon vinegar
1 teaspoon rock salt
½ teaspoon black peppercorns
275 ml (½ pint) olive oil or ground nut oil
Dash of tabasco

Scrub and bake the potatoes (see page 179).

Break the eggs in the goblet of a liquidiser, add the peeled garlic cloves, mustard, vinegar, rock salt and black peppercorns. Cover and blend at high speed for a minute. Have the oil ready in a measuring jug and start adding it in the thinnest possible trickle directly on to the whirling blades. Once about two-thirds of the oil has been added the mayonnaise will be starting to thicken and you will have to stop the machine occasionally to scrape down the sides of the goblet. When all the oil has been incorporated, taste and add a little tabasco.

When the potatoes are baked cut a cross in the top of each, squeeze the sides gently to open up the gash and put a generous spoonful of the aïoli in each potato. Serve hot.

Garlic and Nut Sauce with Baked Potatoes

(*Serves 6*)

6 old potatoes

Sauce:
50 g (2 oz) walnuts
50 g (2 oz) almonds, in skins
2 large cloves garlic, peeled
6 tablespoons olive oil
Generous squeeze of lemon juice
Salt and freshly ground black pepper

Scrub and bake the potatoes (see page 179).

Pour 6 tablespoons of boiling water into the goblet of a liquidiser. Set the machine in motion and gradually feed the nuts, followed by the garlic cloves, on to the whirling blades. Once the nuts are incorporated, add the oil in the thinnest possible stream so the mixture becomes a thick paste. Stop the machine, taste and flavour the sauce with the lemon juice, salt and freshly ground black pepper

When the potatoes are baked cut a cross in the top of each one, squeeze the sides gently to open up the gash and put a generous spoonful of the nut sauce in each potato. Serve hot.

Note: Try this simple recipe for 4 people, if you are left with uneaten jacket potatoes.

3 large baked potatoes
1 onion
3 sprigs of fresh thyme
Salt and freshly ground black pepper
10 g (½ oz) butter
10 g (½ oz) lard

Chill the potatoes. Peel the onion and the potatoes and grate them coarsely together in a bowl. Strip the leaves from the thyme and add to the potatoes with salt and freshly ground black pepper.

181

Melt the butter and the lard in a frying pan and press in the potatoes, using a fish slice. Cook for about 10–12 minutes until the underside is a good, crusty brown. Transfer to toast the surface under the grill. Invert on to a serving plate and serve hot.

Potatoes in Spiced Yoghurt　　　　　(*Serves 4*)

450 g (1 lb) potatoes
2 tablespoons oil
½ teaspoon finely chopped fresh ginger
½ teaspoon cinnamon
¼ teaspoon ground cardamom
Good pinch of powdered cloves
2 bayleaves
150 ml (¼ pint) yoghurt
1 teaspoon rock salt
½ teaspoon black peppercorns

Scrub the potatoes thoroughly and boil in salted water until tender. Leave to drain in a colander while you return the pan containing the oil to a low heat. Sprinkle the spices into the pan. As soon as the potatoes are cool enough to handle, slice and return them to the pan. Cook quickly until lightly browned, then turn off the heat and add the crumbled bayleaves and yoghurt. Cover the pan with a lid, give the contents a good swirl around, then leave on one side, still covered, for a few minutes.

Crush the rock salt and peppercorns together in a pestle and mortar. Spoon the potatoes into a warmed serving dish. Sprinkle with the crushed seasoning and serve.

Potato Gnocchi Baked with Garlicky Tomato Sauce

(Serves 5–6)

Substantial stuff, this, so serve it simply with a green salad. If possible, boil the potatoes whole and resist the temptation to keep testing them to see if they are done or they will become a bit water-logged.

Tomato Sauce:
1 large Spanish onion
2 tablespoons oil
2 × 397 g (14 oz) tins tomatoes
2 fat cloves garlic, crushed
1 bayleaf
1 teaspoon dried basil

Potato Gnocchi:
900 g (2 lb) old potatoes
1 standard (No. 4) egg
25 g (1 oz) butter
175 g (6 oz) wholewheat flour
1 teaspoon baking powder
Salt and freshly ground black pepper
Freshly grated nutmeg

Topping:
50 g (2 oz) grated Parmesan cheese
2 rounded tablespoons dry brown breadcrumbs
25 g (1 oz) butter

Peel and finely chop the onion. Heat the oil in a medium saucepan and gently fry the onion until softened but not coloured. Add the tomatoes, the crushed garlic, bayleaf and basil. Simmer gently, uncovered, for 45 minutes or until you are left with a good pint of sauce.

Meanwhile, prepare the potato gnocchi. Scrub the potatoes and boil them in their skins in salted water until tender. Drain them and leave to cool a little, before peeling and rubbing through a sieve into a bowl. Beat the egg and add with the butter to the sieved potatoes, followed by the flour, baking powder, salt, freshly ground black pepper and freshly grated nutmeg. Taking a handful of paste at a time, roll out on a lightly floured surface to finger-thick long sausage shapes. Cut these into 2·5-cm (1 in) lengths, then pick up in one hand and indent in the centre with the forefinger of the other, so the effect is something like a pillow that has had someone's head resting on it. Arrange the gnocchi in a single layer on a plate.

Pre-heat the oven to 180 °C (350 °F/mark 4).

Bring a large saucepan of salted water to the boil and drop the gnocchi in one by one; do them in batches of about two dozen. They will surface after about 1 minute. Give them another 2 minutes, then fish them out with a draining spoon and arrange in a buttered 2-litre (3½ pint) deep baking dish, layering each batch with tomato sauce and a sprinkling of Parmesan and seasoning as you go. Finish with a layer of gnocchi topped with the remaining Parmesan combined with the breadcrumbs. Dot with butter and bake in the top half of the oven for 30 minutes. Serve bubbling hot with additional Parmesan and yoghurt.

PUDDINGS

Good *English* things, puddings, especially the hot ones. And this, for the main part, is what I have stuck to: English puds, but with a wholefood twist, using brown flour, brown sugar, etc. It is quite incredible how much better they taste for this treatment.

Puddings are the one aspect of our national cuisine for which we were noted, indeed *praised*, but are now almost completely neglected. Mind you, the reasons for this are all too apparent. Just a quick mental flip through the puddings of one's youth will immediately register a more than abundant use of sugar, eggs, suet, butter, flour and cream. As one who puts on weight with aspirins and toothpaste, I can only sympathise with those who fight this constant battle.

I am also sure that in going through that list one or two of you gave an involuntary shudder with sudden recollections of the horrific puddings you were made to eat as a child: slimy, sweet suet puddings; cloggy frogspawn; lumpy custard, and the like. Overcoming this sort of childhood culinary trauma can only be accomplished by taking your courage in both hands and trying the hot puddings in this chapter. When properly made they are not only very good but cheap and filling enough for the most voracious appetites in the family. If these puddings were just an occasional feature, nay highlight, of a week's family menu, it should keep bills and waistlines down and not make too many demands on your time.

As for the cold puddings, I was forcibly struck when testing suitable recipes by the fact that sugar can be kept down to a minimum with no trouble at all. It is far better to use too little than too much sugar, as it can deaden and nullify flavours in no uncertain way—a fact that some of our so-called 'haute cuisine' cookery books have cheerfully ignored. Ultimately, nothing can be more important than flavour.

Orange Soufflé Omelette   (*Serves 1 or 2*)
with Rhubarb Sauce

A nice, simple dish that can be done in fifteen minutes flat, from a standing start. It is also easy to double up on if you want to serve more than two.

Rhubarb Sauce:
225 g (8 oz) rhubarb, trimmed
Brown sugar, to taste

Omelette:
3 large (No. 2) eggs
Grated rind and juice of 1 small orange
1 dessertspoon soft brown sugar
A little unsalted butter

Slice the trimmed, washed rhubarb into short lengths. Put into a pan with half the orange juice, cover and cook gently until reduced to a pulp. Stir in sugar to taste. Keep warm while preparing the omelette.

Separate the eggs, placing the yolks in one bowl and the whites in a separate, grease-free bowl. Whisk together the yolks, grated orange rind, the other half of the juice, and the sugar then, using an absolutely clean, dry whisk, beat the egg whites until stiff and carefully fold into the yolk mixture.

In an omelette pan, heat the butter until frothy. Pour in the egg mixture and cook slowly until the base is set and golden (carefully slip a palette knife under the edge of the omelette and lift gently to see what is going on underneath).

Put the pan under a grill and cook the surface of the omelette.

Have ready a warmed plate dusted with caster sugar. Quickly turn the omelette out on to the plate, pour the rhubarb sauce over it, fold the omelette in half and serve immediately, if not sooner.

Wholewheat Buttermilk Pancakes (*Makes 16 pancakes*)

These are rather delicious, like a lighter version of a Scots (griddle) pancake, but definitely more of a pud than a dish to be served at teatime. Serve with butter and maple or golden syrup, or with home-made damson jam and soured cream.

110 g (4 oz) wholewheat flour
½ teaspoon bicarbonate of soda
¼ teaspoon salt
225 ml (9 fl oz) buttermilk
2 standard (No. 4) eggs

Sift the dry ingredients into a bowl. Pour the buttermilk into a jug and whisk in the egg yolks, putting the whites in a separate, grease-free bowl. Now gradually whisk the buttermilk mixture into the dry ingredients to form a smooth batter. If you are eating the pancakes as a pudding, prepare the batter up to this stage just before you sit down for the meal.

When ready, whisk the egg whites until stiff but not dry, and gently fold into the batter. Transfer the batter to the jug and heat a griddle iron or large, seasoned frying pan. Wipe a minimum of lard or oil over the surface and pour in sufficient pools of batter to give pancakes about 7·5 cm (3 in) diameter; you will probably manage a maximum of 4 at a time. Cook over a heat set just below moderate and they will take about 2 minutes on each side. Flip the pancakes over once the bubbles hold on the surface and the undersides are golden brown. Serve hot.

Prune and Apricot Oatmeal Crumble

(*Serves 6*)

A lovely crumble topping that will of course adapt to practically any fruit, fresh or dried.

225 g (8 oz) prunes
225 g (8 oz) dried apricots
845 ml (1½ pints) boiling water
25 g (1 oz) soft brown sugar
2·5 cm (1 in) cinnamon stick

Crumble Topping:
110 g (4 oz) wholewheat flour
110 g (4 oz) porridge oats
75 g (3 oz) Demerara sugar
2 teaspoons cinnamon
75 g (3 oz) butter
50 g (2 oz) hazelnuts, chopped and roasted

Put the prunes and apricots in a bowl, pour in the boiling water and leave to soak for about 8 hours.

Transfer the soaked fruits and their liquid to a saucepan and add the sugar and cinnamon stick. Bring to the boil, cover and simmer gently for 10 minutes. Uncover and continue to simmer gently until the fruit is plump and tender and the soaking liquid has become a bit syrupy; this will take about a further 10 minutes.

Pour the contents of the pan into a baking dish, discarding the cinnamon stick, and leave to cool while preparing the crumble topping.

Pre-heat the oven to 180 °C (350 °F/mark 4).

Combine the flour, oats, sugar, cinnamon and butter in a bowl. Rub in the butter until the mixture has an even crumb then fork in the hazelnuts. Sprinkle this mixture over the fruit and bake for 40 minutes or until the crumble topping is tinged brown and some of the juices have bubbled up to the surface. Serve hot or cold with yoghurt, custard or ice-cream.

Fig Spotted Dick with Rum and Caramel Sauce   (*Serves 5–6*)

This is a lovely combination of flavours that to my mind knocks the boring old Christmas pud and brandy butter into a cocked hat!

225 g (8 oz) dried figs
225 g (8 oz) wholemeal self-raising flour
110 g (4 oz) butter
50 g (2 oz) soft brown sugar
A pinch of salt
2 standard (No. 4) eggs
About 3 tablespoons milk

Rum and Caramel Sauce:
75 g (3 oz) light soft brown sugar
3 tablespoons warm water
150 ml (¼ pint) double or soured cream
About 2 teaspoons dark rum

Liberally butter a 1 litre (2 pint) pudding basin.

Cut the dried figs into small pieces, about the size of your little fingernail, discarding any hard bits of stalk.

Put the flour, butter, sugar and salt into a bowl and rub the fat into the dry ingredients until the mixture resembles fine breadcrumbs. Stir in the fig pieces.

In a separate bowl, beat together the eggs with a tablespoon of milk. Stir this into the crumb mixture, adding sufficient extra milk to allow the mix to drop fairly readily from the spoon; this should not need much more than a further 2 tablespoons of milk. Transfer the mix to the buttered bowl and level off the top with the back of a spoon. Butter a double thickness of foil, one side only, and fold a pleat in the centre. Line the pleat up across the centre of the pudding (buttered side down!) and secure firmly down under the rim of the basin with string. Steam over gently-boiling water for 2½ hours.

To make the sauce, put the sugar in a smallish saucepan. Heat and allow the sugar to melt and begin to darken. Stir, and when liquid and slightly darkened (about the colour of a ginger biscuit), immediately turn off the heat and, standing well clear, add 3 tablespoons of warm water. The mixture will splutter and bubble up quite a bit. When the ferment has subsided, return the pan to the heat and boil gently for a further 1 minute. Remove from the heat and leave to cool slightly. Stir in the cream and some rum to taste. Warm gently.

When the pudding is ready, discard the foil and string, loosen the pudding round the edge with a palette knife and turn out on to a heated serving plate. Serve hot with the sauce.

Wholemeal Sponge-Topped Plum Pud
(Serves 6)

A fairly quick pudding to make because it uses the 'one-stage' method: the sponge ingredients all go into the bowl at once and are beaten until smooth. If you do not believe this, try it.

900 g (2 lb) plums
Rind and juice of 1 orange
1 teaspoon cinnamon
1 rounded tablespoon soft brown sugar

Sponge Topping:
225 g (8 oz) wholemeal self-raising flour
110 g (4 oz) margarine, at room temperature
110 g (4 oz) soft brown sugar
2 large (No. 2) eggs
1–2 tablespoons milk
1 tablespoon chopped almonds
1 tablespoon Demerara sugar

Pre-heat the oven to 180 °C (350 °F/mark 4)

Halve the plums, remove the stones and put the fruit in a 2 litre (3½ pint) deep baking dish. Grate the rind from the orange into a separate mixing bowl; squeeze the juice and sprinkle over the halved plums with the cinnamon and brown sugar. Turn the fruit over to coat in the flavourings.

To make the topping, simply put the flour, margarine, sugar and eggs into the bowl containing the orange rind. Beat together until smooth, then add sufficient milk to give a soft, dropping consistency. Blob dollops of the mixture on top of the fruit, then spread evenly with the back of a spoon. Sprinkle the surface with the almonds and Demerara sugar and transfer the dish to a baking sheet in the centre of the oven for 45–60 minutes, or until the pudding is golden and cooked through in the centre. Serve hot or cold with a real egg custard.

Spiced and Fruited Brown Rice Pudding

(*Serves 6*)

Again, just a wholefood variation of an old standard, but what a difference! It bears no relation whatever to most people's stock ideas of a rice pudding; either so stiff you could stand a spoon up in it or so wet that a plate can hardly contain it!

110 g (4 oz) dried apricots
175 g (6 oz) pitted prunes
250 g (9 oz) brown rice
About 720 ml (1¼ pints) milk
3 tablespoons dark brown sugar
1 standard (No. 4) egg, beaten
½ teaspoon cinnamon
Freshly grated nutmeg

Topping:
About 250 ml (8 fl oz) creamy yoghurt
1 tablespoon dark brown sugar

Soak the dried fruits overnight. The following day, drain and chop them.

Put the rice in a sieve and sluice under the cold tap for a minute. Leave to drain thoroughly while you bring the milk to the boil. Stir in the rice, then cover and cook over a low heat for about 50 minutes or until the rice is tender. As rice varies in amount of liquid it will absorb while cooking, it may be necessary to add a little more milk before the rice is finally tender.

Pre-heat the oven to 180 °C (350 °F/mark 4).

When the rice is cooked remove the pan from the heat and stir in the sugar, beaten egg, cinnamon and nutmeg.

Butter a 2·25 litre (4 pint) ovenproof casserole. Put a layer of half the rice mixture in the base and cover with a layer of half the chopped fruits. Spread the remaining rice over the top and cover with a final layer of the remaining fruit. Cover the casserole with a lid and bake in the oven for 30 minutes. Remove the pudding from the oven. Lightly beat the yoghurt with a fork to make it smooth, then spread over the surface of

the pudding. Sprinkle with the additional tablespoon of dark
brown sugar and serve warm or cold.

Brown Bread and Butter   (*Serves 6*)
Pudding with Fluffy Cider Sauce

This takes the humble bread and butter pudding right up into
the gourmet class! Please use home-made bread: this may
sound like a counsel of perfection to some but I have found
that shop-bought bread used in puddings produces a frankly
slimy result.

4 tablespoons rum
110 g (4 oz) sultanas
About 12 slices home-made brown bread
Butter
570 ml (1 pint) milk
150 ml (¼ pint) single cream
1 vanilla pod
75 g (3 oz) soft brown sugar
5 standard (No. 4) eggs, beaten

Cider Sauce:
3 egg yolks
50 g (2 oz) light soft brown sugar
150 ml (¼ pint) dry cider

Pre-heat the oven to 180 °C (350 °F/mark 4)

Warm the rum in a small saucepan, stir in the sultanas and
leave to plump up.

Trim the crusts from the bread and butter the slices; cut
each slice in four.

Butter a deep, 2 litre (4 pint) baking dish. Arrange layers of
buttered bread in the dish, interspersing each layer with some
of the sultanas and rum.

Put the milk and cream into a pan (the rum one will do!),
add the vanilla pod and heat slowly to just below boiling point.
Remove the pan from the heat, discard the vanilla pod and
stir in the sugar.

Have the eggs, ready beaten, in a bowl. Pour in the hot milk mixture, stirring quickly, and pour this, in turn, over the bread in the dish. Transfer the dish to sit in a roasting tin and pour tap-hot water into the tin. Put carefully in the oven to bake for 50–60 minutes or until the top is golden brown and deliciously crisp.

To make the sauce, simply whisk the egg yolks and sugar together in a heatproof bowl until light and fluffy. Sit the bowl over a pan of barely simmering water and continue to whisk, gradually adding the cider as you do so. Continue to whisk for 8–10 minutes to give the egg yolks a chance to cook and thicken the sauce. Serve in a warmed bowl with the pudding.

Flamri with Fresh Raspberry Sauce
(Serves 6)

Strange-sounding ingredients, but a delicious result.

Flamri:
275 ml (½ pint) home-made dry white wine
110 g (4 oz) semolina
110 g (4 oz) light soft brown sugar
3 standard (No. 4) eggs, plus 1 extra standard (No. 4) egg
  white

Sauce:
450 g (1 lb) raspberries
A little lemon juice
Icing sugar

Pre-heat the oven to 150 °C (300 °F/mark 2)

Liberally butter a 1 litre (2 pint) deep baking dish (I usually use a soufflé dish).

Put the wine into a medium saucepan with 150 ml (¼ pint) of water. Bring to the boil and stir in the semolina. Continue cooking and stirring until thickened then turn down the heat and leave to cook for 5 minutes more. Remove the pan from the heat.

In a bowl combine the sugar with one whole egg and 2 egg yolks, putting the whites in a separate grease-free bowl. Whisk the sugar and egg mixture until thick and fluffy, then gradually beat in the semolina, a little at a time to avoid producing a lumpy mixture.

Combine all three egg whites and, using a clean whisk, beat until stiff but not dry. Fold this into the semolina mixture, then scoop into the prepared dish. Sit the dish in a roasting tin, transfer to the oven and pour tap-hot water into the tin. Bake for 45–60 minutes or until the pudding is slightly puffed and set in the centre. Remove the dish from the water and leave until cooled to lukewarm. Loosen the side of the flamri from the dish and invert on to a serving plate. Leave the dish sitting over the flamri while it chills in a fridge.

To make the sauce, rub the raspberries through a nylon sieve into a bowl. Taste and sharpen the purée with a little lemon juice, then sweeten with the minimum of sieved icing sugar.

Remove the dish from the chilled flamri and serve with some of the raspberry sauce spooned over, the rest to be served at the table.

Chilled Honey, Cream and Nut Dessert

(*Serves 4–6*)

Very rich and rather delicious! Each portion is served surrounded by chunks of fresh fruit, so that you eat the cream part with a spoon and the fruit by hand. All must be thoroughly chilled so a fridge is a necessary prerequisite!

275 ml (½ pint) double cream
225 g (8 oz) mixed nuts: brazils, walnuts, hazelnuts, cashews, almonds (unsalted!)
225 g (8 oz) Greek honey, or any other clear, good-quality unblended honey

Per person:
1 banana
1 clementine
75–110 g (3–4 oz) grapes, or any selection of fresh fruits available
Additional honey, to serve

Have the cream and a bowl chilling in the fridge with small ramekins or individual serving dishes.

Put the nuts on a baking sheet and *lightly* toast under the grill, then leave to cool. Chop coarsely.

Pour the honey into a bowl and, using an electric hand whisk if possible, whip until it is the pale-blonde biscuit colour of evaporated milk, then transfer to the fridge.

Prepare the fruit, segmenting the clementines, halving and pipping the grapes but leave the bananas until ready to serve.

Pour the chilled cream into the chilled bowl and whisk until it will hold a shape. Fold in the honey, but not completely, so blonde streaks of it are discernible in the cream. Fold in all but 2 tablespoons of the chopped nuts in two or three strokes only. Chill for 1 hour minimum.

When ready to serve, put the chilled ramekins on small plates and surround with the prepared fruits and the freshly-sliced banana. Pile the honey and cream mixture in the ramekins. Drizzle a little additional honey over the top and sprinkle with the reserved nuts. Eat and enjoy!

Hellenic Syrup-Soaked Cake   (*Serves 6*)

This cake is baked in a ring mould and has a fruit-flavoured syrup poured over it as soon as it is cooked. It needs at least 24 hours to absorb the syrup throughout the cake so bake preferably 2 days in advance.

3 large (No. 2) eggs
75 g (3 oz) light soft brown sugar, sieved
150 g (5 oz) margarine or butter, at room temperature
75 g (3 oz) plain wholewheat flour
25 g (1 oz) ground almonds
1½ teaspoons baking powder
75 g (3 oz) semolina
Grated rind and juice of 1 large orange

Syrup:
225 g (8 oz) light soft brown sugar
5 cm (2 in) piece cinnamon stick
Juice of 2 large oranges
Juice of 2 lemons
25 g (1 oz) candied orange peel, chopped
1–2 tablespoons brandy

To Serve:
Clotted cream
Toasted, slivered almonds

Pre-heat the oven to 180 °C (350 °F/mark 4)

Butter a 1¼ litre (2½ pint) ring mould.

Separate the eggs, putting the whites in a large grease-free bowl and the yolks in something similar. Whisk the egg whites until stiff but not dry, then gradually whisk in *half* the sugar and continue to whisk until stiff.

Put the margarine or butter and the remaining sugar in the bowl containing the egg yolks. Beat until light and fluffy. Fold in the flour, ground almonds, baking powder and semolina alternately with the orange juice, then the rind. Fold in the egg whites and transfer the mixture to the greased ring mould. Bake in the centre of the oven for 35 minutes.

While the cake is baking, prepare the syrup. Put the sugar

in a pan with 150 ml ($\frac{1}{4}$ pint) of water and the cinnamon stick. Bring to the boil, then adjust the heat so the syrup boils gently for 5 minutes. Remove the pan from the heat and add the fruit juices and peel.

When the cake is cooked turn it out on to a warmed serving dish. Bring the syrup back to boiling point, add the brandy and pour over the cake (it will seem an awful lot of syrup but do not worry, the cake absorbs it). Cool, then cover with cling film and leave in a cool place for a minimum of 24 hours. Serve with clotted cream and sprinkled with toasted, slivered almonds.

Petits Mont Blancs (Serves 6)

This is my own version of a French classic. The meringue base can be used and adapted for many other sweets and the brown sugar gives it a lovely flavour.

Meringues:
3 large (No. 2) egg whites
75 g (3 oz) castor sugar
110 g (4 oz) brown sugar

Chestnut Topping:
350 g (12 oz) chestnuts
150 ml (¼ pint) milk
1 vanilla pod
50 g (2 oz) light soft brown sugar
1–2 tablespoons single cream
275 ml (½ pint) whipping cream
Grated chocolate, to decorate

Pre-heat the oven to 140 °C (275 °F/mark 1)

Put the egg whites in a clean, grease-free bowl. Whisk until they form soft peaks, then gradually whisk in the castor sugar, a tablespoonful at a time. Once all the castor sugar has been incorporated and the meringue forms stiff peaks, sieve the brown sugar into the bowl. As brown sugar is fairly sticky stuff, it will need a bit of persuading through the sieve but it will go. Fold it into the meringue with a metal spoon.

Have ready a large baking sheet lined with oiled silicon paper. Spread out six equal dollops of meringue to rounds of about 13 cm (5 in) diameter. Bake in the centre of the oven for 1½ hours, then switch off and let the meringues stay inside until the oven is cold.

To prepare the topping, nick each chestnut using a small, sharp knife. Put them in a saucepan with cold water to cover. Bring to the boil and boil gently for 10–15 minutes. Take out a few at a time and peel off the outer shells and the inner skins.

Return the peeled chestnuts to the rinsed-out pan and pour in the milk, 275 ml (½ pint) of water and add the vanilla pod. Bring to the boil, then simmer gently, partially covered with a lid, for 30 minutes. By this time the chestnuts should be absolutely tender; drain and place in a bowl.

Heat the sugar and 150 ml (¼ pint) of water slowly in a small saucepan until the sugar has dissolved. Turn the heat up and continue until the syrup reaches 115 °C (236 °F) or the soft ball stage when a small amount of the syrup dropped into cold water will form a soft, pliable ball.

Immediately pour the syrup over the chestnuts, beating vigorously (preferably with an electric hand whisk). Beat in sufficient cream to soften the paste slightly.

Whip the cream and chill until ready to serve. At that stage, spread the cream over the meringue bases and rub the chestnut paste through a nylon sieve directly on to each meringue so that it is piled high with soft vermicelli-like strands of chestnut. Grate a little chocolate over each one and transfer to a flat serving dish.

Honey, Cream and Walnut Tart   (*Serves* 6)

This is a wholewheat pastry tart shell filled with a fudgy, high-density walnut mixture. These sort of tarts are usually too sweet; this one is not. The finished tart looks best served either with blobs of cream around the edge and one in the centre, or, if you can run to it, spread the entire surface with cream and sprinkle with a little chopped caramel.

Pastry Case:
See Leek and Curd Cheese Flan (page 69)

Filling:
175 g (6 oz) walnut pieces
50 g (2 oz) light soft brown sugar
75 ml (3 fl oz) good-quality clear honey
150 ml (¼ pint) double cream
6 level tablespoons soured cream
2 standard (No. 4) eggs
Whipped cream, to decorate

Pre-heat the oven to 200 °C (400 °F/mark 6)

Prepare and line a 24 cm (9½ in) flan tin with the pastry (see page 69). Bake for 20–25 minutes or until firm and lightly browned around the rim; remove from the oven and leave to cool.

The walnut pieces need only slight chopping.

Combine the sugar and 3 tablespoons of water in a medium pan and bring slowly to the boil. Once all the sugar has completely dissolved, boil briskly until the syrup is a deep caramel colour. Remove the pan from the heat immediately and add the walnuts, honey and creams. Return to the heat and stir until the mixture boils; boil briskly for 2 minutes then remove from the heat. Leave to cool for 5 minutes.

In a bowl whisk the eggs, then quickly stir into the walnut mixture. Return to cook over a low heat and, once the first few bubbles of the boiling mixture break the surface, remove the pan from the heat and spread the mixture in the tart shell. Leave until cold, then chill in the fridge for about 2 hours before serving, decorated with whipped cream.

Rum and Raisin Yoghurt Mould   (*Serves 6*)

These flavours marry up well with pears so I usually serve this mould turned out on a large plate, surrounded by peeled and quartered pears that have been poached in a sugar syrup until tender. Spoon a little cream over the top and sprinkle the pears with skinned and chopped pistachio nuts if you really want to go to town. The sort of dish that winds up a family Sunday lunch very nicely.

1 dessertspoon gelatine
3–4 tablespoons dark rum
75 g (3 oz) raisins, stoned
50 g (2 oz) soft brown sugar
275 ml (½ pint) single cream
275 ml (½ pint) home-made yoghurt

If you are using the old-fashioned type of sticky, squashy, stoned raisins you will need to chop them a little before starting. If you have the sort of raisins that are about the same size as sultanas, chopping them will be unnecessary.

Spoon the rum into a small saucepan. Stir in the raisins and gelatine powder and leave aside for 5 minutes while you lightly oil an 845 ml (1½ pints) mould. Heat the rum mixture very gently until it becomes liquid and clear again. Stir in the sugar, continue to heat gently for a further minute, stirring all the time, then remove the pan from the heat.

Stir the cream and yoghurt together in a bowl and when smooth add the rum mixture. Leave aside until cooled and just beginning to set, then stir and pour into the prepared mould; this makes sure that all the raisins remain evenly distributed throughout the mixture. Chill until firm.

When ready to serve, dip the mould briefly in hot water, free the side and invert on to a serving dish.

Dried Apricot Sorbet   (*Serves 6–8*)

If given the choice between fresh or dried apricots, I would choose the dried version every time because they are so infinitely adaptable in cookery. They have a marvellous flavour that lends itself to a whole variety of sweet and savoury dishes, cakes and even preserves. Here, they make a delightful sorbet which I usually serve in individual bowls or glasses with a little apricot brandy spooned over the top, and accompanied by home-made, crisp little biscuits like macaroons or almond tuilles.

225 g (8 oz) dried apricots
75 g (3 oz) soft brown sugar
Juice of 1 large lemon
2 egg whites
50 g (2 oz) almonds, unblanched

Put the apricots in a large bowl, pour in 845 ml (1½ pints) of water and leave to soak overnight. Pour the contents of the bowl into a saucepan, bring to simmering point, then cover and cook gently for 10–15 minutes or until the apricots are tender.

Have a nylon sieve ready over a bowl; decant the contents of the pan into the sieve. Measure the juice drained from the apricots and make up to 275 ml (½ pint) with water if necessary. Return the juice to the pan and add the sugar. Bring slowly to the boil, and once all the sugar has dissolved, boil gently for 2 or 3 minutes. Pour the syrup, apricots and lemon juice into the goblet of a liquidiser and blend until the mixture is reduced to a smooth purée. Pour the purée into a bowl and freeze until mushy.

While the sorbet freezes, toast the almonds on a baking sheet in the oven for about 15 minutes at 180 °C (350 °F/mark 4). Cool a little then chop, not too finely.

When the sorbet has reached the mushy stage, remove from the freezer and beat (preferably with an electric hand whisk), until lightened in colour and a uniform icy-smooth consistency. In a separate bowl, using a clean, dry whisk, quickly beat the egg whites until stiff but not dry. Fold the egg whites and the toasted almonds into the apricot purée and return to the freezer to chill until firm.

Transfer the sorbet to the main body of the fridge for about an hour before serving.

Wholemeal Bread Iced Cream   (*Serves 6*)

This is rather delicious with a lovely nutty, caramel flavour—and very rich.

570 ml (1 pint) double cream
50 g (2 oz) vanilla sugar
2 tablespoons brandy
175 g (6 oz) wholemeal bread
175 g (6 oz) soft brown sugar

Pre-heat the oven to 200 °C (400 °F/mark 6)

Put the cream, vanilla sugar and brandy together in a large bowl and whip until the cream will just hold a shape. Transfer to the freezer. When the cream begins to harden around the edge, stir the outside into the middle.

Meanwhile, crumb the bread and sprinkle evenly over a large well-oiled baking sheet. Sprinkle the brown sugar over the top and bake in the centre of the oven for 15 minutes. At this stage, check how far the sugar has melted and caramelised. It needs to go as brown as possible without the sugar actually burning and going bitter. In my oven it will usually take another 5 minutes but it needs regular checking as ovens vary quite a lot. Remove the baking sheet and leave to cool. Break up the crumb and sugar mixture and transfer to a deep bowl. Using the end of a rolling pin, pound up the pieces to reduce them to crumbs again. When the cream mixture is semi-stiff, fold in the crumbs, then re-freeze until firm.

Half an hour before serving scoop the iced cream into individual serving dishes and transfer to the main body of the fridge. This gives the cream a chance to soften and mellow a little before eating.

Four Star Dried Fruit Compote   (*Serves 6*)

I always think it is a daft tradition to serve a rather solid Christmas pudding to follow what is usually an enormous main course. A much better idea is to serve a lighter, sharper, fruity compote like this and keep the Christmas pud for Boxing Day. Pine nuts are used in this recipe; if these prove difficult to get, substitute hazelnuts.

110 g (4 oz) giant prunes
110 g (4 oz) dried apricots
110 g (4 oz) dried figs
275 ml (½ pint) white port
50 g (2 oz) raisins, stoned
50 g (2 oz) pitted dates
50 g (2 oz) whole almonds
50 g (2 oz) walnut pieces
50 g (2 oz) pine nuts
Grated rind of 1 large orange
Juice of 2 large oranges
About 2 heaped teaspoons dark brown sugar
Yoghurt or cream, to serve

Sluice the prunes, apricots and figs with cold water and put in a saucepan with the port. Bring to boiling point, cover and simmer gently for 5 minutes. Draw off the heat and leave covered and undisturbed for about 8 hours, or overnight.

The following day snip the prunes in half to remove the stones. Snip off the stalks and halve the figs. Return the fruit to the port with the raisins and halved dates.

Blanch and halve the almonds; coarsely chop the walnuts and add to the fruit with the pine nuts, orange rind and juice.

Lastly, dissolve the sugar in two tablespoons of boiling water and stir into the compote. Cover and leave aside for a further 8 hours. Serve lightly chilled with yoghurt or cream.

CAKES, BISCUITS
AND BREAD

This is the department from which I derive most satisfaction. I challenge anyone not to feel a real 'Mrs. Goodsorts' glow of satisfaction when surveying a selection of breads, biscuits and cakes that are the products of an afternoon spent baking in the home.

Baking is particularly rewarding as far as wholefoods are concerned because the results of using such ingredients as brown flours and sugar are nothing like those you can buy in a shop; and the flavours are home-made, fresh and superb. Nowhere is this more strongly highlighted than in the case of bread. I heard just recently that 75 per cent of the population actually prefer white, sliced bread. Who are these people? If this is the case, all I can say is that civilisation has gone into over-drive! To taste bread as it should be, bake your own; experience the extraordinary satisfaction that comes from kneading dough; feel that almost sensual pleasure in handling it, and smell the perfume of the baking loaf. Finally, sit down and eat a slice of the freshly-baked bread, spread with butter and home-made lemon curd.

I rest my case!

Wholefood Currant Cheesecake

(*Serves 12–16 slices*)

Before going any further it must be made clear that this cheesecake sinks in the middle; I have never yet come across a cooked cheesecake worth its salt that doesn't. It is more of a cake than a pudding which is why it is here in the baking section and not the pudding part. Ideally it should be baked in what the Americans call a 'spring-form pan'. This is best described as a cake tin with a detachable waist band: the side comes away from the base by undoing a sort of buckle arrangement. But it is perfectly possible to bake the cheesecake in an ordinary cake tin, solid, or with a removable base.

Crumble for base and sides:
200 g (7 oz) digestive biscuits
50 g (2 oz) walnut pieces, finely chopped
75 g (3 oz) soft brown sugar
½ teaspoon cinnamon
75 g (3 oz) butter

Cake:
350 g (12 oz) curd cheese
175 g (6 oz) soft brown sugar
4 standard (No. 4) eggs, separated
150 ml (¼ pint) soured cream
50 g (2 oz) wholewheat flour
Rind of 1 lemon, finely grated
2 teaspoons lemon juice
110 g (4 oz) currants
25 g (1 oz) wheatgerm
A little icing sugar

Pre-heat the oven to 170 °C (325 °F/mark 3)

Crush the digestive biscuits and put in a bowl with the finely chopped walnuts, sugar and cinnamon. Rub the mixture together between your fingers, as you would for making pastry, to break down any lumps of sugar. Melt the butter and work it evenly into the crumble, using your fingers in the same manner.

Liberally butter a 20 cm (8 in) cake tin. Press the crumble

thickly on to the side of the tin using the back of a tablespoon—this sounds impossible but it will stay put. Press the remaining crumble evenly on the base of the tin.

In a large bowl beat together the curd cheese and sugar until smooth. Add the egg yolks, then the rest of the ingredients in the order listed above. In a separate bowl whisk the egg whites until stiff but not dry, and fold into the mixture carefully. Pour into the prepared cake tin and bake for $1\frac{1}{2}$ hours with the top of the tin level with the centre of the oven, and a sheet of greaseproof paper laid on top. Turn the heat off and let the cheesecake stand in the oven for a further hour.

Remove the cake and leave on a rack to cool for a further 4 hours. If not using a spring-form pan, loosen the side with a palette knife, invert the cheesecake on to one plate, then again on to a serving dish to bring it right side up. Dust with icing sugar and serve.

Roseleen's Carrot Cake

This always raises a few eyebrows but it really *works* and makes a light, moist, spongey cake. Wherever Roseleen got the recipe from I don't know, but I thank her.

3 medium carrots, about 200 g (7 oz)
175 g (6 oz) soft brown sugar
205 ml (7 fl oz) ground nut oil
2 standard (No. 4) eggs, beaten
225 g (8 oz) plain wholewheat flour
1 teaspoon bicarbonate of soda
1 teaspoon cinnamon
110 g (4 oz) walnuts, chopped

Topping:
110 g (4 oz) full fat soft cream cheese
50 g (2 oz) unsalted butter, at room temperature
50 g (2 oz) icing sugar, sieved

Pre-heat the oven to 150 °C (300 °F/mark 2)

Brush a tin 28 × 18·5 × 4 cm (11 × 7 × 1½ in) with melted fat. Line the base with greaseproof paper and brush the paper with fat.

Scrub, trim and coarsely grate the carrots; you should end up with 175 g (6 oz). The cake is simplicity itself to make: put the grated carrots in a bowl and beat in the other ingredients one after the other in the order listed above, sifting in the dry ingredients. Spread the mixture in the prepared tin and bake in the centre of the oven for 40 minutes or until the cake is nicely risen, firm to the touch and has begun to shrink away slightly from the sides of the tin. Leave to cool in the tin and turn out on to a wire rack when only just warm.

The topping is just as simple to make as the cake. Beat all the ingredients together until the mixture is smooth. Spread over the top of the cake and leave to firm up a little in a cool place before dividing into squares and serving.

Fresh Ginger Cake with Date Filling

This cake is made with fresh ginger which a few of the large supermarket chains are now selling as a regular thing. It gives a lovely round, positive flavour to a nicely moist cake.

150 ml (¼ pint) milk
2 teaspoons lemon juice
75 g (3 oz) soft margarine
75 g (3 oz) soft brown sugar
1 large (No. 2) egg
275 g (10 oz) wholewheat flour
1½ teaspoons bicarbonate of soda
150 g (5 oz) treacle
150 g (5 oz) honey
75 g (3 oz) fresh ginger, peeled and finely grated

Filling:
225 g (8 oz) pitted dates
Juice of ½ lemon
3 tablespoons water
A little icing sugar

Pre-heat the oven to 180 °C (350 °F/mark 4)

Brush a tin 29 × 18 × 4 cm (11½ × 7 × 1½ in) with melted fat and line with greaseproof paper, then grease the paper as well.

Measure the milk into a measuring jug and stir in the lemon juice to sour the milk. Put aside in a warm place.

Put the margarine and sugar together in a bowl and cream until light and fluffy. Break the egg into a separate bowl and beat with a fork before gradually beating into the creamed mixture, a little at a time. Sift the flour and the bicarbonate of soda together, and fold in alternately with the soured milk, followed by the treacle, honey and grated fresh ginger. Spread the mixture evenly in the tin and bake in the centre of the oven for about 1 hour or until the cake shows signs of shrinking away from the sides of the tin. This cake will be absolutely flat when baked. Remove from the oven and leave to cool in the tin for about 15 minutes before turning out on to a wire rack.

To make the filling, simply put the dates in a small saucepan with the lemon juice and water. Cover and cook gently for about 5 minutes. Uncover and beat vigorously so the dates are reduced to a readily spreadable paste.

Cut the cake in half down the middle to give two rectangles. Spread the date paste on one half, turn the other half top side up and position on top. Sift a little icing sugar over the surface and serve.

Date, Apple and Walnut Loaf with Fudge Frosting

A cake with an icing but, if your energy deserts you before the frosting is made, it is delicious plain, just cut in thick slices and spread with butter.

110 g (4 oz) pitted dates
110 g (4 oz) walnut pieces
110 g (4 oz) butter or margarine, at room temperature
175 g (6 oz) soft brown sugar, sieved
2 standard (No. 4) eggs, beaten
225 g (8 oz) plain wholewheat flour
1 teaspoon baking powder
1 teaspoon cinnamon
½ teaspoon ground cloves
2 medium cooking apples

Fudge Frosting:
225 g (8 oz) soft brown sugar
170 ml (6 fl oz) carton single cream
50 g (2 oz) butter
About 2 tablespoons walnuts, chopped

Pre-heat the oven to 180 °C (350 °F/mark 4)

Butter a 1¼ litre (2½ pint) loaf tin.

Chop the dates and walnuts.

In a large mixing bowl cream the butter and sugar until pale and fluffy. Add the beaten eggs, a little at a time, beating well between each addition. Using a metal spoon fold in the flour, baking powder and spices, followed by the chopped dates and walnuts. There is no need to peel the apples. Coarsely grate them directly into the bowl and fold in. Transfer the mixture to the prepared tin and level the surface with the back of a spoon.

Bake in the centre of the oven for 1 hour or until the loaf feels springy in the centre and a thin skewer inserted in the middle comes out clean. Leave the cake to cool in the tin for 5 minutes before turning out on to a wire rack.

To make the frosting, put the sugar and cream together in a

saucepan and stir over a low heat until all the granules have dissolved, then bring to the boil, cover with a well-fitting lid and boil steadily for 3 minutes. Remove the lid and continue to boil until the syrup reaches soft-ball stage at 115 °C (238–239 °F), when it will form a soft, pliable ball when dropped into cold water. Remove the pan from the heat and beat in the butter. Continue beating until the frosting is thick enough to coat the cake without flowing off it. Put the cake on a serving dish and quickly smooth the frosting over it. If it seems too thick, add a little water to the frosting. Scatter the cake with additional chopped walnuts if you wish.

Dried Fruit and Nut Fingers

Pastry:
225 g (8 oz) wholewheat flour
2 teaspoons baking powder
110 g (4 oz) margarine

Filling:
150 g (5 oz) currants
150 g (5 oz) sultanas
110 g (4 oz) glacé cherries
110 g (4 oz) walnut pieces
75 g (3 oz) soft brown sugar
1 large (No. 2) egg
25 g (1 oz) bran flakes
110 g (4 oz) margarine or butter

Pre-heat the oven to 180 °C (350 °F/mark 4)

Lightly grease a large swiss roll tin.

Make the pastry in the usual way by rubbing the fat into the dry ingredients. Add just sufficient cold water to combine the mixture to a non-sticky dough that leaves the side of the bowl clean. Roll out and use to line the swiss-roll tin, bringing the pastry up to the edge. Trim off any excess and use to fill any gaps in the edges. Crimp attractively all round the edge.

Make the filling by combining the dried fruit, chopped nuts, sugar and bran in a bowl. Break the egg into a separate bowl, beat lightly with a fork and pour over the dried fruit mixture.

Melt the margarine or butter gently in a small saucepan, cool and stir this in also. Smooth the filling on to the pastry-lined tin and bake on the shelf below centre for 30 minutes. Cover with a sheet of foil and continue baking for a further 10 minutes. Leave to cool and cut into bars or squares before turning out on to a wire rack.

Peanut Butter Biscuits

(Makes about 28 biscuits)

These are extremely simple to make, indeed they are just the sort of thing that children can tackle in the kitchen. Everything goes together into the one bowl, is mixed, formed into balls, flattened slightly and baked. I use the crunchy type of peanut butter, but the smooth stuff works just as well. Note to peanut butter loathers like myself: these biscuits are very nice!

75 g (3 oz) margarine at room temperature
110 g (4 oz) peanut butter
110 g (4 oz) soft brown sugar
175 g (6 oz) wheatmeal flour
1 small (No. 6) egg
¾ teaspoon bicarbonate of soda
¼ teaspoon salt
Demerara sugar

Pre-heat the oven to 180 °C (350 °F/mark 4)

Lightly grease a baking sheet.

Put all the ingredients, except the Demerara sugar, in a bowl and mix into a stiff dough. Form the mixture into walnut-sized balls; there is no need to roll in flour or anything as the mixture is dry enough to leave the hands clean.

Tip a small heap of Demerara sugar on to the work top and place a ball of mixture in the sugar; flatten it off slightly, flip it over and place sugared-side up on a lightly-greased baking sheet. The biscuits will end up about 6·5 cm (2½ in) diameter, so allow enough room for expansion during baking.

Bake in the centre of the oven for 15–20 minutes or until the biscuits feel firm when tested with the fingertips. Leave to cool and harden on the baking tray for 3 or 4 minutes before transferring to a wire rack with the aid of a palette knife. Cool and store in an airtight container.

Poppy Seed Bars (*Makes 20 bars*)

Is it a cake or is it a biscuit? I do not know, it is one of those things that is impossible to decide one way or the other. Anyway, they are rather different and rather delicious.

50 g (2 oz) butter or margarine at room temperature
75 g (3 oz) soft brown sugar
2 standard (No. 4) eggs
1 teaspoon vanilla extract
175 g (6 oz) wholemeal flour
1½ teaspoons baking powder

Topping:
150 g (5 oz) soft brown sugar
150 g (5 oz) poppy seeds

Pre-heat the oven to 180 °C (350 °F/mark 4)

Brush a small swiss-roll tin, base measurement 18 × 28 cm (7 × 11 in), with melted fat. Line the tin with greaseproof paper, allowing the paper to come up a good 2·5 cm (1 in) above the tin and grease the paper.

Beat the butter or margarine until softened, add the sugar and beat until hard again, lightened in colour and fairly fluffy in texture.

Separate the eggs, placing the whites in a clean, grease-free bowl. Beat the yolks and vanilla extract into the creamed mixture, then stir in the flour and baking powder. The mixture will now be too dry to hold together and will look rather like fresh brown breadcrumbs. Sprinkle this into the prepared tin and level it off with the back of a spoon.

Set a liquidiser in motion and pour the measured amount of poppy seeds in a steady stream on to the whirling blades. Continue to blend for about a minute until the poppy seeds resemble a coarse-textured flour, then stop.

Whisk the reserved egg whites until stiff but not dry, then gradually add the brown sugar and continue to whisk until the meringue will hold firm peaks. Fold in the pulverised poppy seeds and spread the mixture evenly over the biscuit base.

218

Bake in the centre of the oven for 25–30 minutes or until the meringue has browned lightly and the mixture has shrunk slightly from the sides of the tin. Remove from the oven and leave in the tin until cold before cutting into bars or squares. Remove from the tin using a palette knife and store in a tin.

Macaroons, Wholefood Style
(*Makes about 3 dozen biscuits*)

These are lovely, easy little biscuits to make and are about the one and only occasion on which I would condone the use of a piping bag! Please read the notes beneath the recipe before you start.

110 g (4 oz) whole almonds, unblanched
110 g (4 oz) soft brown sugar
110 g (4 oz) Demerara sugar
10 g (½ oz) ground rice or semolina
2 standard (No. 4) egg whites
Blanched almonds, to top each biscuit
Rice paper, to line baking sheets

Pre-heat the oven to 150 °C (300 °F/mark 2)

Use a nut mill or mouli grater to grind the almonds into a bowl. Add the sugars and ground rice or semolina and mix well before stirring in the egg whites.

Transfer the paste to a large piping bag fitted with a plain ½ cm (¼ in) piping nozzle. Have ready baking sheets lined with sheets of rice paper. Pipe out the rounds of paste about the size of a 50p coin (imagining it to be round!) and allow space for expansion between each biscuit. Place a blanched almond on top of each biscuit.

Bake in the centre of the oven for 30 minutes. Leave to cool on the baking sheets before lifting the biscuits off (you may need the aid of a palette knife, particularly if the biscuits had to wait before going into the oven). Tear off the rice paper surrounding each biscuit and leave to cool completely before storing in an airtight tin.

Notes: This recipe can be adapted to make walnut, hazelnut, pine nut or even (perish the thought!) coconut biscuits. Simply substitute the 110 g (4 oz) almonds for whatever you choose. Like the almonds, the hazelnuts need not be peeled.

If you prefer the biscuits rather chewy, leave them out overnight and store in an airtight container the following day. These biscuits are useful if made very small: no bigger than a 5p piece. They can then be used for topping off trifles in the traditional way, for petit fours after a rather grand dinner party, or as nibbles with drinks around Christmas time.

Bran and Sesame Biscuits   (*Makes about 4 dozen*)

These are a chewy cross between a digestive biscuit and a crispbread and are good with cheese, delicious spread with butter and honey, or just eaten plain, on their own. Normally I go for speed and don't bother to cut them out into fancy shapes, just squash the dough out very thinly (*very* important) and cut it into crispbread-shaped rectangles, or squares or diamonds, so it is rather difficult to say how many biscuits this quantity makes but I would guess at about 4 dozen 5 cm (2 in) squares.

110 g (4 oz) fine oatmeal
110 (4 oz) wholewheat flour
25 g (1 oz) bran flakes
½ teaspoon salt
55 ml (2 fl oz) groundnut oil
1 level tablespoon clear honey
About 25 g (1 oz) sesame seeds

Pre-heat the oven to 180 °C (350 °F/mark 4)

Butter a large baking sheet.

Combine the oatmeal, flour, bran flakes and salt in a bowl. Mix the oil, honey and 55 ml (2 fl oz) water together in a separate bowl and add just enough of this mixture to combine the dry ingredients into dryish, crumbly dough. Pat the dough out on the buttered baking sheet and then roll it out as thinly as possible, no more than 3 mm (⅛ in) thick. If all your baking sheets have a rim around them that does not allow you to roll the dough out quite this thin with a rolling pin, use a jam jar, or some other short, cylindrical object instead. Sprinkle the surface of the dough with the sesame seeds and roll again to press them into the surface. Score the dough into squares or diamonds, and bake in the top half of the oven for 12–15 minutes. Turn out on to a wire rack and leave to cool before storing in an airtight container.

Wholewheat Shortbread   (*Makes 8 wedges*)

I never make the conventional shortbread now, just this one.
If you fancy a really crunchy version, the cornflour can be
substituted with the same amount of semolina.

50 g (2 oz) soft brown sugar
110 g (4 oz) butter, at room temperature
25 g (1 oz) cornflour
150 g (5 oz) plain wholewheat flour
1 tablespoon Demerara sugar

Pre-heat the oven to 170 °C (325 °F/mark 3)

Grease a baking sheet.

Put the first four ingredients in a bowl and work with a hand
or spoon until the ingredients come together to form a smooth
dough. Turn out on to a lightly-floured surface and knead
gently to form a smooth round. Roll out to a round of about
2·5 cm (1 in) thick. Transfer the round to the greased baking
sheet and finish rolling out the dough to between ½–1 cm (¼–
½ in) thick 23 cm (9 in) diameter actually on the baking sheet.
It is done this way because the fully rolled-out dough is too
fragile to pick up and transfer from work surface to baking
sheet. Pinch the edge between thumb and forefinger, then
prick the centre all over with a fork. Mark into wedges and
sprinkle with the Demerara sugar. Bake in the centre of the
oven for 30 minutes or until the shortbread is firm when tested
lightly with the fingertips in the centre. Remove and leave to
cool for 5 minutes before cutting into wedges with a sharp
knife. Transfer to a wire rack to cool. Store in an airtight tin.

Barley and Cider Rolls (*Makes 12 rolls*)

225 g (8 oz) barley flour
225 g (8 oz) strong white, unbleached flour
1 teaspoon salt
25 g (1 oz) butter or margarine
2 teaspoons brown sugar
150 ml ($\frac{1}{4}$ pint) hand-hot water
10 g ($\frac{1}{2}$ oz) fresh yeast or 2 teaspoons dried yeast
150 ml ($\frac{1}{4}$ pint) dry cider

Combine the flours and salt in a bowl. Rub the fat into the dry ingredients.

Pour the correct amount of hand-hot water into a measuring jug and stir in the sugar. If you are using fresh yeast, crumble it into the liquid, stir and use immediately. If using dried yeast, stir it into the liquid and then leave aside for 10–15 minutes or until the liquid has a good 2·5 cm (1 in) of frothy head on it and the granules have completely dissolved. Pour the yeast liquid and cider on to the dry ingredients and mix to a soft dough. Turn out on to a lightly-floured surface and knead for about 10 minutes, until smooth and no longer sticky. Place the dough in a clean bowl and enclose in an oiled plastic bag. Leave to rise in a warm place for about 1 hour, until doubled in volume.

Flour a baking sheet.

Punch the air out of the risen dough and knead again until elastic, about 2 or 3 minutes. Divide the dough into 12 equal pieces and shape each one into a ball. Place the rolls, almost touching, on a well-floured baking sheet. Dust the tops with additional barley flour then enclose the baking sheet in an oiled plastic bag and leave in a warm place to prove for about 35 minutes, until the rolls are puffy and have joined together.

Pre-heat the oven to 220 °C (425 °F/mark 7) about 20 minutes before the rolls are due to be baked. Bake for 20–25 minutes or until golden brown and crisp. Separate out and leave to cool on a wire rack.

Quick Bran Loaf

This loaf is quick to make because you need only wait for the dough to rise; there is no shaping or proving. It is a good recipe for the tentative bread maker to start with or for children to tackle.

400 g (14 oz) wheatmeal flour
50 g (2 oz) unprocessed bran
1½ teaspoons salt
25 g (1 oz) butter or margarine, at room temperature
2 teaspoons black treacle or malt extract
355 ml (12 fl oz) hand-hot milk and water, mixed
10 g (½ oz) fresh yeast or 2 teaspoons dried yeast

Grease a large 900 g (2 lb) loaf tin.

Place the flour, bran and salt in a bowl. Rub the fat into the dry ingredients.

Pour the correct amount of hand-hot mixed milk and water into a measuring jug and stir in the black treacle or malt extract. If using fresh yeast, crumble it into the liquid, stir and use immediately. If using dried yeast, stir it into the liquid and leave aside for 10–15 minutes or until the liquid has a good 2·5 cm (1 in) of frothy head on it and the granules have completely dissolved. Stir the yeast liquid into the dry ingredients to form a slightly moist dough.

Place the dough into the well-greased loaf tin. Smooth the top, then enclose the tin in an oiled plastic bag and leave in a warm place for about 30 minutes, until the dough has risen to the top of the tin.

Pre-heat the oven to 200 °C (400 °F/mark 6) about 20 minutes before the loaf is due to be baked. Bake for 45 minutes. To test if the loaf is cooked turn it out of the tin and it should sound hollow when tapped on the base. Cool on a wire rack before eating.

Boozy Bap

This is a good keeping loaf.

350 g (12 oz) wholemeal flour
110 g (4 oz) plain unbleached flour
1½ teaspoons salt
50 g (2 oz) lard
1 tablespoon honey
150 ml (¼ pint) hand-hot water
10 g (½ oz) fresh yeast or 2 teaspoons dried yeast
150 ml (¼ pint) brown ale

Combine the flours and salt in a bowl. Rub the lard into the dry ingredients.

Pour the correct amount of hand-hot water into a measuring jug and stir in the honey. Once it has dissolved, if you are using fresh yeast, crumble it into the liquid, stir and use immediately. If using dried yeast whisk it into the liquid with a fork, then leave aside for 10–15 minutes or until the liquid has a good 2·5 cm (1 in) of frothy head on it and the granules have completely dissolved. Pour the yeast mixture and brown ale on to the dry ingredients and mix to form a soft dough. Turn it out on to a lightly-floured surface and knead for about 10 minutes, until smooth and elastic. Place the dough in a clean bowl, enclose it in an oiled plastic bag and leave in a warm place for about 1¼ hours, to rise until doubled in volume.

Flour a baking sheet.

Punch the air out of the risen dough and once again knead it until firm and elastic. Flatten the dough into a 20 cm (8 in) round and make a slight hollow in the centre. Transfer to the well-floured baking sheet, enclose in an oiled plastic bag and leave for about 40 minutes until almost doubled in size.

Pre-heat the oven to 220 °C (425 °F/mark 7) about 20 minutes before the loaf is to be baked. Bake for 30 minutes until golden and the bread sounds hollow when tapped on its base. Cool on a wire rack before eating.

Herby Brown Soda Bread

A good, quick recipe for the occasions when you are desperate for bread. The flavourings can be varied to suit the food with which the bread is to be served but basil, marjoram and thyme do seem to be about the best. Don't forget that some of the seeds are excellent too: cummin, fennel, caraway and dill, etc.

225 g (8 oz) wholewheat flour
225 g (8 oz) unbleached plain white flour
¾ teaspoon salt
1 teaspoon bicarbonate of soda
2 teaspoons cream of tartar
1 teaspoon honey or brown sugar
½ teaspoon dried marjoram
½ teaspoon dried basil
¼ teaspoon dried thyme
50 g (2 oz) butter or margarine, at room temperature
275 ml (½ pint) buttermilk, yoghurt or sour milk

Pre-heat the oven to 190 °C (375 °F/mark 5)

Flour a baking sheet.

Put all the ingredients into a large bowl, except the buttermilk (or alternatives). Rub the fat into the dry ingredients until thoroughly blended with the flour. Mix in the buttermilk and stir to form a soft dough.

Turn out on to a work surface lightly sprinkled with wholewheat flour, knead lightly and shape into a round. Transfer to a floured baking sheet. Score the dough into four across the top and leave aside for 5 minutes.

Bake in the centre of the oven for 30 minutes. When cooked, the bread should be well risen and sound hollow when tapped on the base.

If you prefer a slightly less crusty finish on the bread, wrap the loaf in a clean cloth for 10 minutes while it cools. Serve warm and if possible eat the same day as baking, although it can be kept a little longer if well wrapped in self-clinging clear plastic film.

Oatmeal Bloomer

225 g (8 oz) rolled oats or medium oatmeal
225 g (8 oz) strong, white unbleached flour
1½ teaspoons salt
25 g (1 oz) lard
2 teaspoons brown sugar
275 ml (½ pint) hand-hot water and milk, mixed
10 g (½ oz) fresh yeast or 2 teaspoons dried yeast

Place the oats, or oatmeal, flour and salt in a bowl. Rub the lard into the dry ingredients.

Pour the correct amount of hand-hot water and milk mixture into a measuring jug and whisk in the sugar using a fork. If using fresh yeast, crumble it into the liquid, stir and use immediately. If using dried yeast, whisk it into the liquid with a fork then leave aside for 10–15 minutes or until it has a good 2·5 cm (1 in) of frothy head on it and the granules have completely dissolved. Mix into the dry ingredients to form a soft dough. Turn it out on to a lightly-floured work surface and knead for 6–10 minutes, until it is no longer sticky. Place the dough in a clean bowl and enclose the bowl in an oiled polythene bag. Leave in a warm place for about 1½ hours, until doubled in volume.

Flour a baking sheet.

Using your clenched fist, punch the air out of the risen dough then turn out on to the work surface and knead again until firm and elastic. Shape the dough into a rounded baton, about 23 cm (9 in) long and transfer to the well-floured baking sheet. Using a sharp knife, score a series of diagonal cuts on the top of the dough. Enclose the baking sheet in a large, oiled plastic bag and leave in a warm place to prove for about 30 minutes, until the dough has almost doubled in size.

Pre-heat the oven to 220 °C (425 °F/mark 7) about 20 minutes before the loaf is to be baked. Bake for 35 minutes until golden and the bread sounds hollow when tapped on the base. Transfer to a wire rack to cool.

Wholemeal Hazelnut Cob

This is especially good with home-made preserves or cheese.

450 g (1 lb) wholemeal flour
1½ teaspoons salt
25 g (1 oz) lard
175 ml (6 fl oz) hand-hot water
2 teaspoons brown sugar
10 g (½ oz) fresh yeast or 2 teaspoons dried yeast
1 small carton hazelnut yoghurt
50 g (2 oz) hazelnuts

Combine the flour and salt in a bowl. Rub the lard into the dry ingredients.

Pour the correct amount of hand-hot water into a measuring jug and whisk in the sugar with a fork. If using fresh yeast, crumble it into the water, stir and use immediately. If using dried yeast, whisk it into the water, then leave aside for 10–15 minutes until the liquid has a good 2·5 cm (1 in) of frothy head on it and the granules have completely dissolved. Stir the hazelnut yoghurt into the yeast mixture and mix into the flour. Turn the dough out on to a lightly-floured surface and knead for about 6–10 minutes, until it looses its stickiness and becomes smooth. Place the dough in a large clean bowl, enclose in an oiled polythene bag and leave to rise in a warm place for about 1¼ hours, until doubled in volume. While the dough is rising roughly chop the hazelnuts and flour a baking sheet.

Using your clenched fist, punch the air out of the risen dough before turning it out again on to a work surface. Knead for a couple of minutes before gradually working in the chopped nuts. Form the dough into a ball and place on the well-floured baking sheet. Pat the dough to flatten it a little, then score a cross on the top of it using a sharp knife. Enclose the baking sheet in an oiled plastic bag and leave again in a warm place to prove for about 45 minutes, until almost doubled in size.

Pre-heat the oven to 220 °C (425 °F/mark 7) about 20 minutes before the loaf is to be baked. Bake for 35 minutes or until well browned and crisp and the bread sounds hollow when tapped on the base. Transfer to a wire rack to cool.

Index

233

237